A Kid's Guide to

Arab American
History

Praise for *A Kid's Guide to Arab American History*

"Chock-full of fascinating insights into a vibrant, inspiring community, punctuated by fun (even delicious) activities, this book taught me so much! Every American kid should read it, and every American grown-up, too."

—Cynthia Leitich Smith, author of *Jingle Dancer*

"Yvonne Wakim Dennis and Maha Addasi have woven a rich tapestry of the Arab American experience for young readers. History, achievements, trails blazed, challenges faced, and material and social culture—all of it is rendered accessible through the stories of people and communities, some familiar and others much less well known. Numerous craft activities engage attention and imagination by tapping the senses."

—Uma Krishnaswami, author of *The Grand Plan to Fix Everything*.

"*A Kid's Guide to Arab American History* is the ultimate eye-opening introduction to Arab Americans! The authors have skillfully combined informative, engagingly written text with an impressive variety of imaginative crafts and activities from each of the Arab countries, suitable for elementary-age children. This book is just right for families, schools, and anyone who values the incredible richness of our immigrant American nation."

—Elsa Marston, author of *Figs and Fate: Stores About Growing Up in the Arab World Today*

"This book is a delight to read; offering much-needed insights about our neighbors, Americans with Arab roots who have contributed so very much to our society."

—Dr. Jack G. Shaheen, author of *Guilty: Hollywood's Verdict on Arabs After 9/11*

"With its focus on interesting hands-on activities and fascinating profiles of notable as well as ordinary Arab Americans, this book will definitely help dispel many negative stereotypes. It's a much-needed resource that highlights the rich and diverse histories, traditions, cultures, and religions of the most dominant Arab American groups in the US. I highly recommend it."

—Jama Rattigan, author of *Dumpling Soup*

A Kid's Guide to

ARAB AMERICAN HISTORY

More Than 50 Activities

Yvonne Wakim Dennis and **Maha Addasi**

CHICAGO
REVIEW
PRESS

First edition
Published by Chicago Review Press, Incorporated
814 North Franklin Street
Chicago, Illinois 60610
ISBN 978-1-61374-017-0

Library of Congress Cataloging-in-Publication Data
Dennis, Yvonne Wakim.
   A kid's guide to Arab American history : more than 50 activities / Yvonne
Wakim Dennis and Maha Addasi. — 1st ed.
        p. cm.
     Includes index.
     ISBN 978-1-61374-017-0 (pbk.)
   1. Arab Americans—History—Juvenile literature. 2. Arab Americans—History—
Study and teaching—Activity programs—Juvenile literature. I. Addasi, Maha, 1968–
II. Title.

   E184.A65D46 2013
   973'.004927073—dc23

                                                                    2012035758

Cover and interior design: Scott Rattray
Interior illustrations: Gail Rattray

Printed in the United States of America
5 4 3 2 1

We dedicate this book to the wisdom of children and
our dreams that when they grow up they will "wind the world well."

Contents

Acknowledgments

From Yvonne

The courage of Jack Shaheen and Barbara Nimri Aziz inspired me to write this book, and their guidance and encouragement helped me finish it. Thank you, Dr. Jack, for taking the time to be our professional reader. I am indebted to you, Barbara, for directing me to activities and places I needed to be. Kathleen Brown McNalley and Dawi Winston—you ground me, *wado*. Thanks to my son, Jiman, and friends Angela, Irma, Sharon, Khadija, Arlene, and Luca, and especially my very patient husband, who took over my tasks. Thanks for your attention to detail, Michelle Schoob. Cynthia Sherry—*wado* for doing the right thing with both my books! Your vision and commitment to helping make America the inclusive society it needs to be is remarkable!

From Maha

Thanks to the people who will read this book with an open mind and heart and to my children, who give me the peace of mind to write.

Maha and Yvonne are both grateful to these wonderful folks who filled in the blanks and didn't mind being interviewed and "pumped" for information: Adil Oualim, Akram Khater, Douglas Haddad, Elsa Marston, Jeffrey Saad, Joseph Haiek, Joseph Kassab, Khalil Hachem, Laila Al-Qatami, Liz Behrend, Malika Zarra, Musa Hamideh, Naef Al-Mutawa, Paul Ibrahim, Pauline Kaldas, Ray Saeid, Sarab Al-Jijakli, Naomi Shihab Nye, Helen Zughaib, Hani Shihada, Susan Joseph Kientz.

Note to Readers

My journey started in Kuwait, where I grew up in a mixed Arab and American community with Arab friends who shared the same traditions and foods as my family. I also had American friends who taught me how to build the perfect hamburger, how to furnish a dollhouse, and everything anyone needed to know about Charlie Brown and Snoopy.

Our neighborhood celebrated the national, traditional, and cultural holidays, both Arab and American, like Eid, Thanksgiving, and Easter. I was an Arab Muslim girl who helped untangle Christmas tree lights, sang in the choir, and, one year, played the piano to accompany the choir. I loved it all. When I attended college in the United States, I brought this sense of intercultural exchange and shared it with my college friends, some of whom visited me in the Arab world.

Years later, I had the opportunity to immigrate to the United States and make America my home. My children were born here.

I wanted to keep the balance of Arab and American in their life, which grows ever more challenging. Arabs, Arab Americans, and Arab cultures are often treated in a very negative way in the United States. The idea behind *A Kid's Guide to Arab American History* was to bring to light real Arab American culture and the people who have contributed to the fabric of the United States.

—Maha Addasi

My dear friend and coauthor of many books, Arlene Hirschfelder, and my wonderful husband, Roger Dennis, pushed me to write *A Kid's Guide to Arab American History*. Over the years, I had become more angry and dismayed at the untruths and stereotypes aimed at Arabs and Arab American people. For most of my life, I have addressed racism directed at all groups, but particularly First Nations peoples. I am fortunate to be both Indigenous American and Arab American, two of the most misrepresented peoples in history! Through my books, I have tried to set the record straight about Native peoples; it is time to do the same regarding Arab Americans. Much like the Hollywood Indian, who was violent and not too smart, Arab Americans are portrayed as unrealistic and unpleasant characters. None of these portrayals resemble anyone in my family or community, people who are hard work-ing, brilliant, loyal, and deeply spiritual citizens. My very Syrian grandparents would be proud that I wrote a book that tells a bit about their history in America, and my very Cherokee/Sand Hill grandparents would be proud that I walk in balance and honor all of my ancestors.

—Yvonne Wakim Dennis

Time Line

800 BCE–1000 CE • Ancient mariners from the Middle East are thought to have traveled to the Americas. They call it *Ard Majhoola*.

Ard Majhoola

1492 • At least one Arab guide, Louis de Torre, accompanies Columbus on his famous voyage to the Americas.

1528 • Moroccan Zammouri guides a Spanish expedition into Florida.

1539 • "Estaphan the Arab," a Moroccan guide, explores the Southwest.

1776 • Private Nathan Badeen, from Syria, dies fighting in the American Revolution.

1777 • The Kingdom of Morocco is the first country to recognize the new United States as a sovereign nation.

1790 • South Carolina rules that Moroccan Arabs living in the state should be treated according to the laws for whites, not the laws for blacks from Africa. However, enslaved Moroccans are not freed, in spite of the law.

1840 • Captain Ahmed bin Naaman from Oman sails into New York Harbor, making him the first Arab delegate to visit the United States—it was the beginning of trade between the two countries.

1850–1920 • Called the Pioneers, the largest group from Greater Syria comes to the United States during these years. Most work in factories or as peddlers, setting up vast trading networks across the nation.

1856 • The US military imports camels to use in military operations in the Southwest. Arab camel drivers are hired and brought to America to work with the animals.

1865 • Over 5,300 Arab/Muslim Americans serve in the Civil War.

1869 • The opening of the Suez Canal in Egypt makes it possible for more people to emigrate from places like Yemen.

1875 • Many Arabs arrive through New Orleans, Louisiana, which provides access to the north and west.

1876 • The Centennial Exposition in Philadelphia attracts Arab merchants, especially those from Palestine. They do so well that many stay and peddle items from the Holy Land.

1890 • Syrians and Lebanese begin to move west. Some are attracted to mining in the Southwest.

1892 • *Kawkab America*, the first Arabic language newspaper in America, begins publication.

1893 • The World's Columbian Exposition in Chicago draws many merchants from the Arab world. Some Arab American families in the Great Lakes area trace their ancestors to these merchants.

1900 • Dr. Tannous Daoud is elected president of the North Dakota Farming Association.

1909 • The Department of Justice rules that George Shishim, a policeman in Venice, California, can become an American citizen. Until this time, few Arabs were allowed to become citizens because the US government considered them Asian and Asians were denied citizenship. Mr. Shishim testified that if he was Asian, so was Jesus Christ, as they had both been born in the same land.

1911 • Ameen Rihani is the first Arab American to publish a novel in the United States, *The Book of Khalid*.

1915 • Al-Rabitah al-Qalamiyah (The Pen Bond), a literary association, was formed in New York City by Kahlil Gibran and friends.

1916 • A number of Syrian and Lebanese Americans join the French army to free Syria from Turkey.

1917 • The Balfour Declaration, issued by the British, supports the founding of a Jewish homeland in Palestine.

1918 • An estimated 14,000 Arab Americans serve in World War I.

Circa 1920 • An Arab American writers' group, the Pen League or Al-Mahjar (immigrant poets), is founded in New York City by Kahlil Gibran and friends.

1923 • One of the most famous books of all time, *The Prophet* by Kahlil Gibran, is published.

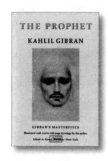

1924 • The United States Immigration Act of 1924 bars immigration from Arab countries.

1929 • The first mosque in America is founded in Ross, North Dakota.

1939–1945 • An estimated 30,000 Arab Americans serve in World War II.

1947–48 • The state of Israel is created, displacing thousands of Palestinians, some of whom come to the United States as refugees.

1948 • Air Force Colonel James "Jabby" Jabara becomes America's first military jet ace pilot.

1949 • Entertainer Danny Thomas founds the American Lebanese Syrian Associated Charities to help raise money for St. Jude's Children's Hospital, which opens in 1962.

1950 • Attorney George Kasem, the first Arab American congressman, is elected.

1965 • The Immigration Act of 1965 removes quotas based on national origin.

1967 • After the third Arab-Israeli war, more Palestinians emigrate to the United States.

1974 • Journalist Helen Thomas becomes the first woman to serve as chief of the White House reporting staff for United Press International.

1976 • Arab Americans protest the inclusion of many words insulting to Arabs in the Merriam-Webster dictionary.

1980 • Former US senator James Abourezk founds the American-Arab Anti-Discrimination Committee (ADC), a civil rights organization that defends the rights of Arab Americans and promotes their rich cultural heritage.

1984 • Engineers Naseeb Saliba and Essam Aly build LAX International Terminal for the Olympic Games held in Los Angeles.

1985 • Thomas Nassif is appointed the US ambassador to Morocco, becoming the first Arab American ambassador.

1987 • The US Supreme Court declares that Arab Americans are protected from discrimination based on ethnicity.

1988 • Arab American senator George Mitchell becomes the US Senate majority leader.

1990 • Some Arab Americans and Muslim Americans are targets of hate crimes as a result of the first Gulf War.

Elias Corey wins the Nobel Prize for Chemistry, the first Arab American to win the award.

1993 • Lucie Salhany becomes chair of FOX Broadcasting Company, making her the first woman to head a broadcast television network. She later goes on to found United Paramount Network.

1999 • Leila Ahmed becomes the first women's studies professor at Harvard Divinity School.

2001 • The Association of Patriotic Arab Americans in Military is founded by Yemeni American Jamal S. Baadani, a gunnery sergeant in the United States Marine Corps.

2002 • The Arab American Institute gives Kahlil Gibran Spirit of Humanity Awards to those Arab American New York City police officers who took part in the rescue efforts of September 11, 2001.

2005 • The Arab American National Museum opens in Dearborn, Michigan.

2010 • Rima Fakih becomes the first Arab American to be crowned Miss USA.

2011 • The first annual Diwan (Forum for the Arts) is held in New York City, uniting Arab American artists, scholars, and performers.

The film *Fordson: Faith, Fasting, Football* shows a predominately Arab American high school football team as they practice, play ball, fast for Ramadan, and deal with the problems of how other Americans see them.

Introduction

Kitty Softpaws has "cat-itude" as she purrs her way into the heart of Shrek's friend, Puss in Boots. Actress Salma Hayek is the voice of the tough glam cat. The iMac, iTunes, iPod, iPhone, and iPad send information, music, and pictures through cyberspace so people can stay in touch all over the world. Steve Jobs invented these little machines. And more machines copy, print, and ship documents around the world at Kinko's (now FedEx Office), founded by Paul Orfalea, who named the company after his curly hair. Because of his learning disability, he didn't do well in school, but today he is one of America's most successful businesspeople. What do these three people have in common? They are all famous. Each was the first to do something in his or her field. And they are all Arab American.

In *A Kid's Guide to Arab American History*, you will come to know not just famous Arab American people, but also the not-so-famous neighbor next door, the owner of the corner store, the mail carrier, or the volunteer firefighter who may be Arab American, too. You will learn about the history, arts, distinctive cultures, and traditions of the many Americans who came from what is known as the Middle East or Western Asia. Arab Americans have contributed to their communities in many ways, including in education, science, health, and entertainment, but Arab inventions and discoveries made it to the Americas, too. Arab Americans come from the people who gave the world the study of social sciences, trigonometry, parachutes, coffee, cameras, universities, cotton, the harp and the bagpipe, navigational aids, maps, books, and surgical tools, to name just a few contributions. Everyday English words such as mattress, sofa, and sugar come from the Arabic language. From the Alamo in Texas to the Citadel in South Carolina, many American buildings reflect Arabic architecture and engineering wonders.

Opa-locka, Florida

This town's name comes from the Indigenous American name for the area, *Opa-tisha-worka-locka*, meaning "a big island covered with many trees and swamps." But the city's architecture is Arabic Moorish, and its streets have names like Sultan and Sesame. One hundred and five buildings boast an array of domes, minarets, and outside staircases. Thousands of buildings throughout the United States are fashioned after Arabic architecture, and Opa-locka is home to more of them than anywhere else in the Western Hemisphere. Twenty of its buildings are on the National Register of Historic Places.

Pick up any newspaper from a newsstand on any given day, and you are guaranteed to see news about the Arab world, most of which is negative. In *A Kid's Guide to Arab American History*, you will learn about real people with Arab roots and how they have contributed to the fabric of the United States. This book will set the record straight. In spite of what the media portrays, Arab Americans are patriotic and loyal to the United States.

Arab Americans may have relatives who still live in Arab countries, may have been born in the Arab world before immigrating to the United States, or may be third- or fourth-generation Arab American. Regardless of how much "Arab" is in Arab Americans, they are all 100 percent American and, like other Americans, still celebrate some customs from the old country. *A Kid's Guide to Arab American History* explores some of these traditions that define Arab American cultures.

This book features people from the countries that are most represented in the United States, such as Lebanon, Syria, Palestine, and Egypt. Because the number of immigrants from Comoros, Djibouti, Mauritania, Sudan, and Somalia is so tiny, Arab Americans from these countries are not included in *A Kid's Guide to Arab Americans*.

In chapter 1, we will learn some basic facts about Arab Americans and their lives in America. You may be surprised to learn of the strong connections between American and Arab cities and probably not too surprised at what is hurtful to Arab Americans. The Maples School Arabic Music Ensemble is featured, and everybody can learn to dance the *Dabkeh*!

Twenty-two countries are considered Arab. They are spread across Western Asia and Northern Africa and have many different climates and cultures. Arabic is their official language. It is also an official minority language in Chad, Eritrea, and Israel, and some immigrants from these countries may be considered Arab as well.

Algeria	Morocco
Bahrain	Oman
Comoros	Palestinian Territories
Djibouti	Qatar
Egypt	Saudi Arabia
Iraq	Somalia
Jordan	Sudan
Kuwait	Syria
Lebanon	Tunisia
Libya	United Arab Emirates
Mauritania	Yemen

Chapter 2 explores Lebanese Americans, the largest Arabic group in the United States. Did you know that the early Phoenicians, ancestors of the Lebanese, sailed around the world? Scooby-Doo shows up, along with animal rights activist Jack Hanna, consumer advocate Ralph Nader, and lots of other people you may not know are Arab American. The very pants you wear may have been made by the Haggar Clothing Company, and those feisty Lebanese textile workers helped win rights for factory workers. Make a *derbekke* drum and whip up a dish of tabbouleh.

Chapter 3 investigates the Syrian American community. Paula Abdul is popular throughout America for her dance moves and appearances on TV shows such as *The X Factor* and *American Idol*. Spend a day with a Syrian American peddler and try your hand at designing a wood-inlay box and a *sarma* embroidered scarf. A game of mancala can be enjoyed with a healthy dish of hummus and pita bread, too. Did you know that Syrian Americans can follow different religious traditions, including al-Muwahhidūn Druze (Druze), Islam, Judaism, Alawi, and Syrian Orthodox?

In chapter 4, you will learn about Arab Americans from Palestine and Jordan. Visit New York City sidewalks to see Hani Shihada's masterpieces, and learn to compose a poem like award-winning poet Naomi Shihab Nye. If you dance the dabkeh, you'll need a dabkeh-inspired vest and a *fatoosh* salad to give you some energy for all that stomping and kicking! Afterward, you can settle in with a good book by Ibtisam Barakat and a good movie by Cherien Dabis. Did you know that an American is queen of Jordan? Palestinian Americans come from the place considered the Holy Land for Christians, Muslims, and Jews.

Egyptian Americans party in chapter 5 at a *Sebou* ceremony for a baby. The Egypt we usually hear about is really old, with pharaohs reigning over the lands. Egyptians are modern folks, too, but you will still enjoy making an ancient-inspired cuff bracelet and playing a game of senet. Turn on the morning news for a glimpse of Egyptian American Hoda Kotb. Sew up a kaftan to wear and light up your path with a *fanous* lantern.

In chapter 6 you'll meet lots of folks who may be Kurds, Jews, Chaldeans, or Arabs, and . . . they are all Iraqi American! Compete in a game of *el-quirkat* and learn about some of the world's earliest inventions and peoples. A copper birthday pendant done up in cuneiform writing is a fashion statement for both boys and girls. Welcome the birds into your yard with an arabesque-designed birdbath and see how Iraqi American Dr. Azzam Alwash is saving the birds and peoples of Iraq.

Yemeni agricultural techniques helped improve American farming, and you will find that and much more in chapter 7 about Yemeni Americans. Did you know the queen of Sheba was an ancient ruler of Yemen? Even that long ago, the Yemeni were growing wonderful crops. Sculpt some fancy coasters inspired by the "wedding cake" architecture frieze designs of Yemen and play a rhyming game of Oh Hillcock, Oh Hillcock.

Chapter 8 sails into *Ard Majhoola*, Arabic for "unknown territory," the name the ancestors of Americans from Morocco, Tunisia, Algeria, and Libya gave America when they first visited centuries before Columbus! Camels arrived in the Southwestern deserts in the 1800s, shocking everyone. Stitch up a camel friend, and make some music on the *karakebs* like Moroccan American musician Malika Zarra. Sew a comfy pair of *belgha* slippers and use them in a Zaida Ben-Yusuf–style portrait picture. Stew up some couscous and serve it on a jasmine plate, showcasing the flower of love. Love was not in the air for some of the first people from the region who settled in America—they were enslaved. Today, you can see the impact they made on American customs.

Many Muslim Americans take a pilgrimage or hajj to Mecca in Saudi Arabia, the holiest of all Muslim places. In chapter 9 you will meet Americans from Saudi Arabia, Kuwait, Bahrain, Qatar, the United Arab Emirates, and Oman. *THE* 99 heroes Jabbar the Powerful and Samda the Invulnerable fly in to show you how to be a comic book superhero author like Dr. Al-Mutawa. Sweeten up your life with some date candy and decorate a Girgian candy bag.

Arab American Quick Facts

- United States Census records indicate that there are almost 4 million Arab Americans, living in all 50 states. However, this figure may be lower than the actual number because Arab Americans have often been counted with other groups.

- The five states with the largest population of Arab Americans are California, Michigan, Illinois, Ohio, and Texas.

- About 94 percent of Arab Americans live in the metropolitan areas of Detroit, Los Angeles, New York, Chicago, and Washington, DC.

- In many states, the majority of Arab Americans are Lebanese.

- In New Jersey, Egyptian Americans are the largest Arab group.

- Syrians are the largest population of Arab Americans in Rhode Island.

- The largest community of Palestinian Americans lives in Illinois, while Iraqi and Assyrian/Chaldean communities are concentrated in Illinois, Michigan, and California.

- Most Iraqi Kurdish Americans live in Nashville, Tennessee.

You will learn the basics of the Islamic religion. Play *Mazen Al Qurawi*, but if you get stuck being "it," don't be anxious, just click your worry beads!

Chapter 10 is a celebration of all things Arab American! Take a trip through the English language with words borrowed from Arabic and visit the countless cities across America with Arabic names. Try your hand at Arabic calligraphy when you make a banner to honor Arab American Heritage Month. Get puffy with Chef Jeffrey Saad's sitti's pancakes—eat them fast, as they don't stay puffy long!

A *Kid's Guide to Arab American History* features the diverse histories and contemporary cultures of Arab Americans. Through hands-on activities, historical accounts, interesting sidebars, and intriguing stories about real people, you will come to a better understanding of Americans with Middle Eastern roots. The back of this book is packed full of information about Arab American organizations, festivals, reading materials, and websites. By the time you finish the book, you will even be able to speak a bit of Arabic. *Quira'a saeedah!*

● 1 ●
Who Are Arab Americans?

"We are proud to present this most talented troupe of elementary children from nearby Dearborn. Ladies and gentlemen, for your listening pleasure, I give you the Maples School Arabic Ensemble!"

As the announcer was finishing, the huge curtain began to rise to the ceiling. Children dressed in traditional Arabic outfits stood on the stage, the bright stage lights glinting off their drums. Their teacher raised her hands, and the centuries-old drum rhythms filled the massive hall, transporting the audience of 2,000 to Sana'a, Baghdad, Cairo, Beirut, and other Arabic cities. The crowd went wild, clapping and moving to the colossal drum sounds created by little hands. The Orchestra Hall, home of the Detroit Symphony Orchestra in Michigan, often came alive with symphonic music, written by Europeans or Americans. Today's performance of "foreign" rhythm-driven tunes from faraway lands was an exotic treat. But these children were American, too, from a school just 20 minutes away. And the music was also American.

Mrs. Catherine Prowse, music teacher at the Dearborn, Michigan, elementary school, founded the group as a way to help kids feel more comfortable and come out of their shells. An Irish American, she learned Arabic music so she could teach her Arab American students to explore and preserve their heritages while studying the many different kinds of music from the Middle East. In her class, boys, girls, moms, and dads all lend a hand with making costumes, instruments, and helping with homework.

The Maples School Arabic Ensemble has members whose families originated in Lebanon, Yemen, Iraq, Syria, Palestine, and Jordan. They have performed in many different places, in different states, and sometimes to raise money for charity. One of the best parts of being in the music group is that students get to write and perform their own drum patterns. The rich traditions brought to the United States from Arab countries will continue to grow and be a part of current music trends.

Did you know that Arab countries are located on two continents? Lebanon, Syria, Palestine (Gaza Strip and West Bank, plus Arab citizens of Israel), Jordan, Iraq, Saudi Arabia, Yemen, Oman, the United Arab Emirates, Qatar, Bahrain, and Kuwait are Arab countries located in the Middle East, or as some geographers call it, West Asia. Morocco, Algeria, Tunisia, Libya, and North Sudan are Arab countries in the northern part of Africa. Most parts of Egypt are in Africa, but part of the Sinai Desert belonging to Egypt is in Asia. The African countries of Sudan, Somalia, Mauritania, and Djibouti are part of the Arab world, too. Some

Arab Americans have ancestors who immigrated to the United States over a hundred years ago, while other Arab Americans were born in their home countries and became naturalized citizens of the United States.

More than 4 million Americans have ancestors from Arab countries. They belong to diverse religious traditions, including Catholic, Melkite, Orthodox, Islam, Druze, and Judaism as well as several different Protestant groups. The vast majority in the United States are Christians whose families came from Lebanon. Ethnic groups such as the Berbers, Kurds, and Chaldeans come from Arabian countries but are not considered Arabs. One can be an Iraqi American but not be an Arab American, as he or she may be a Chaldean or a Kurd.

What do Arab Americans look like? People from Arab countries can have black, brown, or blond hair. They can have brown, blue, or green eyes. Arab Americans are light skinned, dark skinned, and every color in between. Some have straight hair, while others have curly or wavy hair. There are no physical features that define Arab Americans.

Regardless of how they look, many Arabs share similar customs that are universal among Arab peoples as well as some traditions unique to their individual country, town, village, or family. Some Arab Americans speak several languages, including Arabic.

Sister Cities

How would you like to have a sister in another country? American cities have sisters, and many are Arabic. Sister Cities is an international organization that brings people together, city to city. Cities around the world can adopt each other as family and share joint projects, including youth programs to teach kids how to help the environment; create positive change; and encourage friendships and business relationships. Many Arab Americans came from these very places. Here are just a few of the sister cities.

Birmingham, Alabama, and Al-Karak, Jordan

Tempe, Arizona, and Al-Hilla, Iraq

Los Angeles, California, and Beirut, Lebanon

San Francisco, California, and Amman, Jordan

Miami, Florida, and Agadir, Morocco

Elkader, Iowa, and Mascara, Algeria

Chicago, Illinois, and Casablanca, Morocco

Baltimore, Maryland, and Alexandria, Egypt

Minneapolis, Minnesota, and Najaf, Iraq

New York, New York, and Cairo, Egypt

Look in the resource section for a website to find the sister city for your hometown.

This is particularly common among Muslim Arab Americans, who want to make sure their children learn to read the Islamic holy book, the Qur'an, in Arabic. Others only speak English. Some Arab Americans wear the traditional outfits that are worn in their home countries, but most dress like other Americans. People in many Arab countries wear the same kind of clothing as Americans. Certain Arab American Muslims honor their faith by dressing in modest clothing. A number of Arab American Christian clergy marry and have families, as their faith allows, and many wear special clothing. Arab Americans live in all 50 states and work in all kinds of jobs. Many own their own businesses.

Christopher Columbus may have been a latecomer to the Americas! Although most Arab Americans are descended from families who first immigrated to the United States in the 1800s, some historians believe Arabs were visiting the indigenous peoples in the Americas long before there was a United States. They think that inscriptions in New Hampshire's Pattee's Caves, on carved stones in southern Pennsylvania, and in other places may be evidence that Arab adventurers sailed to North America centuries ago.

Guess which country first celebrated the United States winning its freedom from Great Britain? On December 20, 1777, the Kingdom of Morocco formally recognized the United States of America as a sovereign nation. Morocco remains one of America's

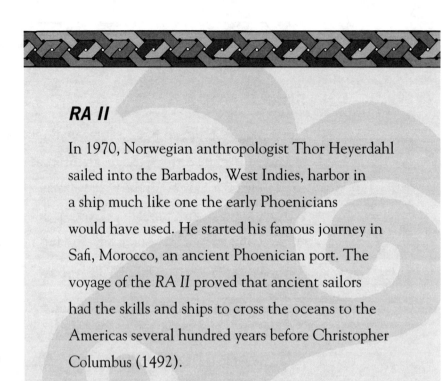

RA II

In 1970, Norwegian anthropologist Thor Heyerdahl sailed into the Barbados, West Indies, harbor in a ship much like one the early Phoenicians would have used. He started his famous journey in Safi, Morocco, an ancient Phoenician port. The voyage of the *RA II* proved that ancient sailors had the skills and ships to cross the oceans to the Americas several hundred years before Christopher Columbus (1492).

oldest and closest allies. Yet, immigrants from Arab countries had a hard time becoming Americans. Some Americans believed that the United States should be a white, Christian country and were intolerant of people from places other than Northern and Western Europe. It took several court battles before Arabs could even become naturalized American citizens, as they were not considered members of the Caucasian race. They were denied citizenship until they pointed out that they were from the same lands where Jesus Christ was born. Arabs prided themselves on their rich language and customs, the very things that white European Americans did not like. Arab Christian rituals were very different from American Christian rites. Muslim and Druze immigrants had an even harder time. It is estimated that almost 20 percent of the first major group to emigrate from the Middle East were Muslim, but they often hid their religion to avoid prejudice.

Most Arab immigrants came between 1890 and 1920. This is known as the first wave of immigration, in which over 250,000 people came to America from Arab countries. They maintained their heritage through their organizations, through their churches, and by starting their own newspapers and publishing companies. They cooked traditional foods and observed their customs around events such as births, deaths, and weddings. Most chose to live close to relatives, as family was the main focus of the Arab American community, as it still is today. They were writers, painters, and musicians. They took jobs in factories and on farms. They traveled coast to coast selling goods to American farms, Indian reservations, small towns, and big cities. Often on foot, men and women carried huge packs of merchandise containing everything from vials of holy water, to socks, to nails. Arab Muslim

immigrants found employment in lumber camps, factories, farms, and livery stables, while Arab Christian immigrants were more likely to become peddlers. This was probably because Christians could quote the New Testament, which appealed to American Christians.

Immigration almost came to a halt in 1924, when the United States passed the National Origins Act, which favored Christian immigrants from Northern and Western European countries, such as England and Switzerland. From 1924 to the late 1940s, few immigrants arrived from Arab countries. The second wave of Arab immigrants began after World War II and continued until the mid-1960s. Most were Muslim; many came as refugees from the 1948 Arab-Israeli War. Others came as college students and applied for citizenship after finishing school.

The third wave of emigration from Arab lands began in mid-1965 after the Immigration and Nationality Act was passed by Congress. The act was supposed to give anyone who wanted to become an American an equal chance. However, even the new act limited who could immigrate to America. Only people with a certain level of education could apply. This is in part why a large number of the newest immigrants are professionals who wanted to get away from the political unrest in their respective countries. Many more are war refugees from Iraq and other countries.

Stereotypes of Arab Americans

How does it make you feel when someone describes an entire group of people as sharing the same characteristics? For instance, "boys are smarter than girls," "poor people are lazy," "Native Americans are not around any longer," or "elderly people do not know much about anything." When people believe that every person in a group is the same, this belief is called a stereotype. TV and movies contribute to the formation of stereotypes, especially in a person who does not know anyone from that group. Stereotypes are hurtful and keep people from becoming friends.

Here are some stereotypes and some truths about Arab Americans.

Stereotype: All Arab Americans come from oil-rich countries.

Truth: Most Arab Americans do not come from countries that are rich in oil. Only the countries around the Arabian Gulf (also known as the Persian Gulf) produce oil, and even in those countries, very few people are rich.

Stereotype: Arab American women have no rights and have to do what men say.

Truth: Arab American women are like any other women in the United States. They work outside the home, own businesses, and create as artists and musicians. Muslim women are guaranteed equal rights by the Qur'an, the Muslim holy book. Non-Muslim women in the Arab world are also guaranteed the same rights as Muslims, as the Bible does not include directions on inheritance and other matters. This demonstrates how Arabs of various faiths live in harmony.

Stereotype: Arab Americans are terrorists.

Truth: People from many backgrounds have committed acts of terror, and most terrorist acts have not been committed by Arab people or involved Arab Americans. In spite of this, people have sometimes jumped to the conclusion that Arab Americans were to blame for all kinds of terroist threats. Some Arab Americans have suffered insults and even violent attacks because of these unfair assumptions. News articles stress terrorist acts in which Arab involvement is known or suspected more than they do terrorist acts performed by other groups. Arab Americans are very loyal to the United States; thousands of Arab Americans have served in the armed forces, at every level, and Arab Americans have fought in every US conflict, including the Revolutionary War. Only Native Americans have a higher percentage of members who have served in the armed forces.

Stereotype: All Arabs come from the desert and ride camels.

Truth: Arab Americans come from countries with different types of climates and many kinds of animals. In fact, camel racing is more popular in Australia than in Arabia.

Stereotype: All Arab Americans are Muslims.

Truth: Most Arab Americans are Christian, and most Arabs who live in Arab countries are Muslim. Some of those who came from or whose ancestors came from Arab countries are Jewish or follow another religion. Only 12 percent of the world's Muslim people are Arab. The country with the largest population of Muslims is the Asian country of Indonesia.

Islam was founded in the Middle East, but so were Christianity and Judaism, as well as some other religions practiced today.

Stereotype: Arab Americans fly around on carpets, carry big swords, and have magic genies in bottles.

Truth: Movies like Disney's *Aladdin* create fairy tales about Arab peoples, but Arab Americans travel like any other Americans and do not have special magic. Arab Americans and Arabs are usually presented in the news, movies, and television as being violent and cruel, but Arab Americans have one of the lowest crime rates of any group.

Stereotype: Arab Americans are poorly educated and speak in pidgin English like in the movies.

Truth: Arab Americans earn twice the number of master's degrees and higher degrees as other Americans. Among foreign-born Arab Americans, most prefer to study the sciences, with large numbers becoming engineers, pharmacists, and doctors. Arab Americans often speak several different languages, which commonly include Arabic, French, and English.

Dr. Jack Shaheen (1935–)

Dr. Jack, a Lebanese American, is a humanist who works hard to debunk stereotypes about all peoples. His book and documentary film, *Reel Bad Arabs: How Hollywood Vilifies a People*, illustrates how Hollywood movies, TV shows, and cartoons have inadvertently shown Arab people as weak and evil villains and have contributed to the discrimination against Middle Eastern Americans. Arab men are made out to be sinister, gun-toting murderers, while Arab women are portrayed as weak and silly. Dr. Jack teaches how these untrue and racist portrayals of Arab people hurt everyone and rob people of their dignity. He also stands up for fair treatment of Asians, Blacks, Latinos, Native Americans, and others. He has been a consultant on Middle Eastern affairs for several news programs as well as movies and television shows. Because of his "outstanding contribution towards a better understanding of our global community," Dr. Jack Shaheen was awarded the University of Pennsylvania's Janet Lee Stevens Award, and the American-Arab Anti-Discrimination Committee's Lifetime Achievement Award in recognition for "his lifelong commitment to bring a better understanding towards peace for all mankind."

Arab Americans participate in all aspects of American society, from rap music, to fashion design, to religion, to government service. Across the country, they still celebrate Arabic culture at festivals, often called *Mahrajan* by Lebanese Americans. Every summer, thousands attend the Arab International Festival in Dearborn, Michigan, the largest Arabic cultural gathering in the nation. Traditional foods, arts, games, and crafts are served up, with everyone joining in a fun-filled line dance called the dabkeh.

Everybody Dance the Dabkeh!

The dabkeh is probably the most famous Arabic dance. It comes from Lebanon, Syria, and other countries nearby. It's danced with the same enthusiasm as the bus stop, hora, or conga. *Dabkeh* means "stomping," so it's important to stomp your foot down really hard! The dabkeh is a lot of fun—look up a Mahrajan in the resources section so you can be part of the festivities.

What You Need

Dabkeh music, purchased over the Internet or listened to on YouTube.

2 or more friends

Open space

What You Do

1. Join hands with the other dancers in the line with your feet slightly apart.

2. Take two steps to your right, one step per beat of the music.

3. Slightly kick your left foot in the air on the third beat. Stomp your left foot on the ground really hard on the fourth beat—this stomping is the most important part of the dance.

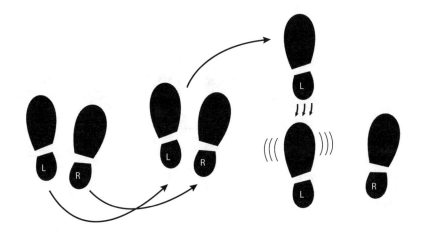

4. Repeat the order of steps, moving to your right for a while. Then change direction and do the same thing to the left. If you're at an Arab event, just follow the leader.

· 2 ·
Lebanese Americans

The White House is all decked out in purple diamonds, gold zigzags, aqua circles, and pink stripes! The door is open to show how welcoming America can be, and a jazzy eagle feathered up in pink, purple, maroon, gold, and black keeps watch over the president's house. The White House has been made into a grand work of art by artist Helen Zughaib, at least in her painting of the famous building! She has created several paintings of the capital's most recognizable landmarks, filling up their blank spaces with pattern and color. Both President Obama and Secretary of State Clinton have given her art pieces as gifts from the American people to visiting world leaders.

Helen Zughaib was born in Beirut, Lebanon, in 1959. Her dad, a naturalized American citizen, was a diplomat for the United States, and the family was stationed all over the Middle East and Europe. She visited great museums and art galleries and learned to knit from her grandmother, who created the most amazing fashions in colorful designs. Helen appreciated how strong women were in Middle Eastern countries and how they healed suffering caused by wars. Helen saw patterns everywhere—in carpets, embroideries, tapestries, buildings, furniture, jewelry. Her unique style and themes come from all these experiences. Another artistic influence was the Arabic tradition of *hakawati*, a series of tales that teach children how to live the right way. Her father shared family stories that had been handed down for generations, and Helen brought them to life in her paintings, retelling the tales in colors and patterns. "The Compassionate Emir" is a story about a leader (emir), his beloved horse, and a wily thief.

The Compassionate Emir

Once an emir owned a famous horse. All who saw the amazing animal were struck by his grace, speed, strength, and beauty. Other emirs were envious and tried to buy the horse, but the owner always refused. Selling the horse, he said, would be like selling a member of his family.

One day a thief spoke to one of the jealous emirs and offered to steal the horse for a price. The bargain was made.

The thief waited by the side of the road where the emir and the wonderful horse passed each day. When the emir approached, the thief began to cry and wail. The emir, who was a kind and compassionate man, stopped to see if he could help.

"What is wrong?" he asked the thief.

"I am very sick," the thief cried.

"Just climb onto my horse, and we will take you to the doctor." The emir reached down to help the man mount the horse.

"I cannot. I am too sick to even climb up." The thief wept and held his stomach.

The emir dismounted and lifted the man onto the horse. As soon as the thief was well seated in the saddle, he kicked the horse and started off at a fast gallop.

The emir called loudly, "Stop and the horse is yours!" The man stopped and returned, knowing that the emir would never go back on his word.

"Do not say you stole this horse," the emir said. "Say that I gave it to you. Do this so that charity and compassion will not disappear from our community."

Perform a Shadow Puppet Show

At one time, coffee houses in Lebanon would compete to see who could feature the best shadow puppet shows. Shadow puppetry is the oldest form of motion picture storytelling and probably originated in China. Lebanese American Julie Taymor is world famous for her remarkable puppets and designed all the characters for the Broadway production of *The Lion King*. Turn "The Compassionate Emir" into a shadow puppet show by writing your own script. You can add more characters if you like.

What You Need

Empty cereal box

Scotch tape

Ruler

Pencil

Scissors

Wax paper

Colored tape

Markers, including black

Paper

Straws

Flashlight or table lamp

What You Do

1. Strengthen the box by covering each end of the box with several pieces of tape.

2. Lay the box on one of its large sides. With the ruler and pencil, measure a rectangle 1½ inches from the outside edge all the way around. Cut out the rectangle. Turn the box over and do the same thing on the other large side. Save the cut-out rectangles for the puppets.

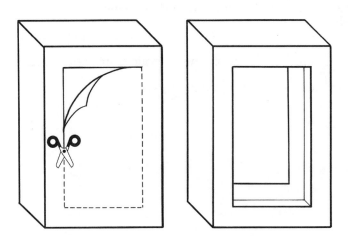

3. Cut a piece of wax paper the same size as the large side of the box. Tape it in place on the inside of the box. The audience will see the side of the box with wax paper.

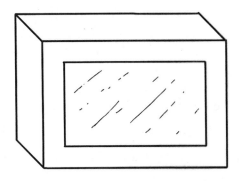

4. Decorate the sides and front of the box with the colored tape and markers, but don't draw on the wax paper.
5. Write a script for your puppets, using the dialogue in the story. You can add characters and dialogue.
6. Use the cardboard from the box to make the puppets by cutting out the shapes of a horse, four emirs, and a thief. You can make trees or other characters, too. Make sure they will fit onto the "stage," which is behind the wax paper. Color your puppets with the black marker. The puppets will be silhouettes. Tape a straw to the back of each—this is what you will hold to move the puppets.
7. Shine the light onto the box from your side of the stage and create your shadow puppet show using the story of "The Compassionate Emir."

15

When civil war broke out in 1975, Helen Zughaib's family had to be evacuated from Beirut. She finished high school in Paris, France, and then moved to the United States, where she studied art at Syracuse University. Her parents had met at Syracuse as students. One of her first jobs was designing china, which helped her develop her particular painting technique.

Today she lives in Washington, DC, where she paints daily; her works have been on display all over the country and are part of permanent art collections around the world. Helen believes that art can create understanding and friendship between Arab countries and the United States.

Jazz Up a Building in Helen Zughaib's Style

Helen Zughaib's works are flat in perspective, packed full of pattern and color, and very well planned. However, Helen is open to surprises. Sometimes after she sketches in the outline and selects her colors, a design she didn't even consider appears. Her motifs are often very American, but with a twist of Arabic that reminds her of their rich heritage. She has been influenced by the varied embroidery traditions of Palestinian women and the diverse designs of Native Americans. Helen uses ink and a type of paint called gouache, which dries very quickly and, once applied, is not as easy to change as oil-based paints are. Her series of famous Washington landmarks honor some of America's most symbolic buildings. Helen's masterpieces are on display at the White House, the World Bank, the Library of Congress, and the Arab American National Museum.

What You Need

An image of a building or buildings you would
    like to paint and ideas for patterns

Scrap paper

Pencil

Watercolor paper

Fine-line ink pen

Tempera paints in red, blue, yellow, black, and white

Containers to mix colors

Fine artist brushes

Container of water for cleaning brushes

Covered work space

What You Do

1. Select a building that is special to you and sketch it on scrap paper.

2. When you are satisfied with your drawing, redraw it on the watercolor paper with the pen and set it aside.

3. Close your eyes for a few minutes; relax and think about colors and patterns. Open your eyes and choose four colors, not including black and white. You can mix the primary colors to get purple, green, or orange and make them lighter or darker with the white and black.

4. Paint in your building with patterns, working as quickly as you can. Try not to think about it too much; just let the patterns and colors take shape. Now, see if other colors and patterns pop into your head. If they do, feel free to add them to your painting.

Helen Zughaib's story is a very different one from that of early Lebanese immigrants—her father was part of the second wave of immigrants. Most Lebanese came to America between 1890 and 1920. Like the Syrians, many made their way by peddling. From trading posts on American Indian reservations, to dry goods stores in big cities, to pack peddling from one prairie town to another, they supplied American customers with everything from nails to underwear. Most Arab Americans are of Lebanese descent.

Imagine yourself on a mysterious journey, crossing mountains, sailing across an ocean with little money, and landing in a place you had only heard about in stories. The Lebanese did exactly that. Some say their great sense of adventure was inherited from their ancestors, the ancient Phoenicians. Known for their brilliant sea navigation skills as well as their remarkable ship-building ability and amazing, far-reaching trade routes, the Phoenicians enjoyed a thriving culture from 6000 to 1000 BCE. They sailed around the African continent and as far north as the British Isles to trade everything from papyrus to their architectural skills. Some evidence suggests they even made it to the Americas!

It was not easy for the Lebanese to leave their long, narrow homeland stretched out beside the Mediterranean Sea. Most came from the forested mountain area called Mount Lebanon, known for the cedars of Lebanon, the very trees mentioned in the Bible and a symbol of the strength of the Lebanese people. Many an immigrant yearned for their sweet smell.

The first Lebanese immigrants to come to the United States were not called Lebanese. Their entry papers noted Turkey or Greater Syria as their country of origin. The modern state of Lebanon did not exist until 1926 and was not completely sovereign until 1943, when it achieved independence from France. Over its long history, the area was invaded and ruled by several different rulers and countries. Sometimes the people were left in peace, but most times the foreign rule caused great problems for the Lebanese and subjected them to poverty. They were often forced to join the ranks of the occupying armies to fight in wars they did not support. Still, the Lebanese loved their homelands, and most left only for better economic opportunities. The Lebanon of today is bordered by Syria, Israel, and the Mediterranean Sea and is about the size of Connecticut, with lowlands, fertile valleys, and a towering mountain range.

Many Lebanese became citizens of the United States, only returning home to visit. Their stories of the lands across the waters so excited the villagers that more and more people emigrated from Lebanon.

The Holy Land Comes to America

What sparked the Lebanese to make such a grand journey? In 1876, Greater Syrian merchants participated in the Centennial Exposition held in Philadelphia, Pennsylvania. They sold crosses, holy water, rosaries, and other religious merchandise. Americans were so thrilled with these wonders from the Holy Land that they bought every single item! The word spread back home and encouraged others from Mount Lebanon to try their luck in the country thought to have "streets of gold." Only a few of them were experienced businessmen, as most educated Lebanese and Syrians emigrated to Egypt and other Arabic countries. So although a few of the early immigrants had schooling, most did not. Peddling was a profession for which one did not need to speak much English or know how to read well, and America seemed to be a place that appreciated Lebanese goods. Some immigrants spoke more than one language, so they learned English quickly. They set up vast trading networks across the country and braved the elements. It wasn't always easy, and some lost their lives trudging around in the harsh winters.

The vast majority of these peddler immigrants were Christian, and this made the transition a bit easier. They were members of the Lebanese Maronite Church, the Melkite Catholic Church, or the Eastern Orthodox Church. Some belonged to various Protestant religions. Many communities dated back to the time of Jesus and the apostles. However, Lebanese Christian rituals were different from those of American churches, and Americans thought them quite strange. Although the Lebanese made their way to almost every state, the majority settled in Northeastern cities.

HO HO HO!

Lebanese American **Robert George (1924–1998)** portrayed Santa Claus year-round for nearly 50 years and was a Presidential Santa at the White House for seven administrations. He owned 38 custom-made Santa suits!

Fashion, Fabrics, and Factories

The Lebanese worked well on their own, as they were independent people, and they worked hard to make a better life. Many had managed their own small farms or run cottage industries. A cottage industry is a home business, and at one time, the Lebanese, like the Syrians, thrived in the silk industry. Women raised silkworms at home, and factories sprung up across Lebanon to spin the raw silk into thread. But a mulberry tree disease broke out, destroying the food source for the silkworms. Then Asian countries began to produce silk for cheaper prices, and the industry dried up. But Lebanese Americans have always influenced the American and international fashion industry and textile production.

In 1920 Mansour Farah and his wife began making shirts in Texas. By 1947, his small home business had grown into the international clothing company Farah Incorporated. Today men's pants are called "slacks" thanks to Joseph M. Haggar. He was another Lebanese American from Texas who turned his little business into the largest manufacturer of men's slacks in the world. Alfred Shaheen took the beautiful batik fabrics of Native Hawaiians and turned them into modern fashions like the popular Hawaiian shirt and the sarong. After flying combat missions in World War II, he returned to Hawaii and, in 1948, founded his own company. In recognition of his contributions to the state of Hawaii, in July of 2001 Alfred Shaheen was presented with Hawaii's Lifetime Achievement Award.

Norma Kamali's famous designs are on permanent display at the Metropolitan Museum of Art in New York City, and Reem Acra's have dressed celebrities such as Angelina Jolie, Beyoncé Knowles, Eva Longoria, and Vanna White. Her flagship store is located in Manhattan.

Become a Fashion Designer

Years ago, paper dolls were as popular as regular dolls and came with their own clothes, but kids often designed outfits from wallpaper samples, gift wrap, or even fabric scraps. If you can find some images or samples of Hawaiian-inspired fabrics, try your hand at designing like Alfred Shaheen. Or you can make fancy gowns like Reem Acra. Or just design your own originals and come up with a whole new style, like they did!

What You Need

Poster board or lightweight
    cardboard
Images of people in swimwear or
    undergarments,
    about 6 to 12 inches tall—
    you can draw them,
    cut them out of magazines,
    use photographs,
    or print from the computer
Scissors

Glue
Poster board
Pencil
Colored markers
Drawing paper
Construction paper
Any of the following: fabric
    scraps, wallpaper samples,
    magazine pictures of fabrics,
    sequins, glitter

What You Do

1. Select images for your paper dolls, making sure they match one another in scale. Cut them out and glue them to poster board. When the glue is dry, cut out your dolls.

2. Make a sketch of your fashion creation on the drawing paper.

3. Pick out some fabrics, images of fabrics, or colors of construction paper. Add glitter or sequins if you want.

4. Lay your paper doll on the fabric. Draw the clothing to fit your doll, shaping it to look like your design. Cut out your design, making sure to leave tabs at the shoulders and other places as needed so you can attach the clothing to the doll.

5. Draw in any details you like with the markers. If you would like your girls and women to have a matching scarf, hijab, or hat, draw it to fit the head and make an opening for the face. Make tabs to attach to the head. You can make a headband or hat for a boy, too. Add accessories such as shoes and jewelry.

While some Lebanese created manufacturing businesses or became fashion designers, others took jobs in textile factories and helped in the struggle for labor rights. In 1912, one of the most famous worker uprisings, called Bread and Roses, took place in Massachusetts textile mills. The slogan Bread and Roses meant that workers needed more pay (bread) and also to be treated with dignity (roses). A new state law had given workers a shorter workweek, and angry factory owners lowered pay. Over 20,000 textile employees went on strike, including women and children. Not only did Lebanese Americans help organize strikes, Arab American women strikers ran soup kitchens to feed their fellow strikers. It was the first time non-Arab workers had ever tasted Lebanese dishes like tabbouleh. The strikers were triumphant and showed the world that semiskilled workers, many of them new immigrants and half of them women, could make a difference.

Cook a Tabbouleh Salad

Tabbouleh, traditionally made with bulgur wheat, fresh parsley, tomatoes, onions, and a squeeze of lemon juice, originated in Lebanon. Bulgur wheat, the grain in tabbouleh, has been eaten for about 4,000 years. It is made from soaking or cooking wheat berries, then drying them and smashing them into tiny pieces. In 2009, 250 Lebanese chefs made it into the Guinness World Records when they cooked up a tabbouleh salad weighing almost 4 tons! It was served in a special ceramic bowl, 20 feet in diameter, designed by Lebanese engineer Joe Kabalan.

What You Need

Adult supervision required

Stove

Small saucepan

$2/3$ cup water

$1/3$ cup bulgur (fine cracked
      wheat)

Bowl

Mixing spoon

1 tablespoon salt

$3/4$ cup freshly squeezed lemon
      juice (about 2 lemons)

$1/2$ cup olive oil

3 tomatoes, diced

1 large onion, peeled and finely
   chopped

1 cucumber, peeled, seeded,
   and diced

2 bunches fresh parsley, finely
   chopped

1 bunch fresh mint leaves, finely
   chopped

Romaine lettuce leaves, separated

Platter

Makes four 8-ounce servings

What You Do

1. In a small saucepan, bring the water to a boil. Remove the pan from the heat and stir in the bulgur. Cover and let stand for 20 minutes, or until all the water is absorbed.

2. When the bulgur has absorbed all the water, scrape it into the bowl. Mix in the salt, lemon juice, olive oil, tomatoes, onion, cucumber, parsley, and mint and refrigerate for at least an hour.

3. Arrange the lettuce leaves on the platter. Scoop up the tabbouleh with the lettuce leaves and enjoy!

Maronite Catholics

It is said that Saint Maron cured the ill and made the sad happy. This monk came to Lebanon from Syria and lived the life of a hermit on Mount Lebanon in the fourth century. After he died, his followers built the Beit Maron Monastery (House of Maron) in his honor and became known as Maronites. The Maronites are the largest of the Lebanese Christian communities and still uphold the same ancient values of living a simple life, building strong supportive communities, and joining in communal prayer. Although they are part of the Roman Catholic Church, their rites are different from those of American and European Catholics.

By 1920 there were almost 40 permanent Maronite parishes in several states, some as far west as California and Oregon, as well as several in New York City, Boston, Philadelphia, and other major cities. Maronite members worked in many different jobs and cities, from the steel factories of Birmingham, Alabama, to the automobile factories of Detroit, Michigan. They opened grade schools for kids and centers to help new immigrants learn English. Today, almost every state has at least one parish. Altogether, there are almost 100 Maronite communities across the nation. Several host festivals to celebrate Lebanese culture, where parishioners and guests alike sample Lebanese food and dance to the rhythms of the *derbekke*.

Construct a Derbekke Drum

A derbekke is a small hand drum popular in Syria, Lebanon, Iraq, Jordan, and Palestine. The drum base is usually vase shaped and made of ceramic or metal with an animal-skin drum head.

What You Need

Adult supervision required

6-inch long or longer rawhide dog bone

Basin or half-gallon pitcher of warm water

Covered work surface

7- to 10-inch tall glass, ceramic, or plastic vase,
    with an opening 4 to 5 inches in diameter

Paint markers, at least 2 different colors

Paper

Pencil

Scissors

Ruler

Heavy-duty shears

Thick, heavy-duty rubber band

What You Do

1. Submerge the dog bone in the water and let it soak until it is soft and pliable, about three to four days. Add warm water every so often. If you can do so easily, unroll the bone after the third day, but put it back in the water until it is really flexible and you can move it easily. This will be the drum head.

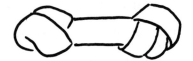

2. The vase will be the drum base. While you are waiting for the rawhide to soak, paint Arabic or other designs on the vase with the paint markers and let it dry.

3. Turn the painted drum base upside down on paper, trace around it, and cut out the traced circle. Put the circle on top of a larger piece of paper. Measuring with the ruler, draw another circle 2 inches larger than the first circle. Cut out this circle. This will be your pattern for the drum head. When the rawhide is pliable, unroll it completely and find a part that is at least 6 inches by 6 inches, with no holes. Do not let the rawhide become dry, or it will be hard to work with. Lay the rawhide flat on the work area and place the circle on top. Trace the circle onto the rawhide and cut it out with the heavy-duty shears. Put the drum head back into the water.

4. Cut a long, thin strip of wet rawhide to secure the drum head to the drum base. Make sure it is long enough to reach all the way around the mouth of the vase with some extra to tie a knot.

5. Take the drumhead out of the water basin and shake off any excess water, but make sure it stays wet. Put the circle on top of the drum base and ask an adult to secure it with the rubber band while you hold it in place, pulling it tightly. Then tie on the rawhide strip over the rubber band as tightly as possible, making sure the top is smooth and taut. Let the head dry before you use the drum. If your derbekke is glass or ceramic, be careful, as it is breakable!

Lebanese Americans and their descendants quickly moved from predominately working as peddlers into all areas of government, the arts, education, science, and business. Many became leaders and inspired other Americans. Artist, philosopher, and poet Khalil Gibran (1883–1931) wrote *The Prophet*, a book of poetic essays that American soldiers often carried in their knapsacks. *The Prophet* is the third-bestselling poetry book of all time. James Abourezk (1931–) was the first Arab American senator (South Dakota) and fought tirelessly for American Indian rights. Journalist Helen Thomas (1920–) was the first woman to head the White House Correspondents' Association, paving the way for American women to enter the field of news reporting. She also started the tradition of wearing a red dress at presidential conferences so she would stand out in the crowd and get the president's attention. Ralph Johns (1916–1997) was a civil rights activist in Greensboro, North Carolina, and that city's first store owner to employ African Americans as salespeople. James J. Zogby (1945–) founded the Arab American Institute and helps build bridges between the United States and Arab countries. Candy Lightner's (1946–) daughter was killed by a drunk driver in 1980. The tragedy motivated her to found the organization Mothers Against Drunk Driving (MADD) so other families could be spared the sorrow of losing a loved one. Everyone knows Ralph Nader, but did you know he is Lebanese American?

The Legend of the Phoenix

Many Americans are from Lebanon's capital, Beirut, nicknamed the Phoenix after an ancient Egyptian story. The phoenix was a bird that would always live to be exactly 500 years old. Then it would make a nest of wonderful-smelling tree bark, such as frankincense and cinnamon, sit in its nest, and burst into flames. The phoenix would die in the fire, but a new bird was reborn from the ashes. This cycle was repeated every 500 years. The phoenix resembled an enormous eagle with beautiful gold and red plumage and sometimes blue and green feathers on its long tail. Like the mythical bird, Beirut keeps rebuilding over and over in spite of being destroyed by wars and invasions. Like the great phoenix, it never dies.

Ralph Nader (1934–)

Ralph Nader is one of the most famous American activists. Through his efforts, laws have been passed to protect consumers and improve car safety. Today, car manufacturers must provide airbags and seatbelts for all vehicles, but at one time these companies were more concerned with profits than safety. Many say that Mr. Nader works harder for the American people than any member of Congress. In 1966, he began to speak out against how abusive big companies were to people and the environment and organized a campaign to force companies to consider consumer and worker safety. Mr. Nader has been responsible for at least eight major federal consumer protection laws, such as motor vehicle safety laws, the Safe Drinking Water Act; and the creation of the Environmental Protection Agency (EPA). A Harvard Law School graduate, he could have chosen a path of wealth and luxury, but instead he lives a simple life, has never owned a car, and is said to be the most vigilant citizen in America. Not only has Mr. Nader helped scores of Americans by insisting the government enact policies to protect consumers, but he has also been available to individuals, average people who had no voice. Mr. Nader ran for president of the United States three times.

Design a National Safety Month Poster

Ralph Nader has spent his life campaigning for safety for people and a clean environment. June is National Safety Month. Make a poster of safety hints in the shape of a phoenix. Like Ralph Nader, be a champion for the environment by recycling used cardboard.

What You Need

Covered work surface

Pencil

Notepaper

Used cardboard boxes, backs of old posters,
 and other used heavyweight paper stock

Stapler

Thin black markers

Poster paints in red, gold, blue, and green

Paintbrushes

Water for washing brushes

Paper hole punch

String (for hanging)

What You Do

1. Sketch an eagle-like bird with outspread wings on the notepaper. When you are satisfied with your design, copy your phoenix onto the used cardboard, making it as large as you can. You can make the head, body, wings, and tail on separate pieces and staple them together.

2. Draw in the feathers. Make them large enough so you can write one safety tip on each feather. Trace each feather with black marker and set it aside to dry.

3. Write down all your ideas for safety on the notepaper: Don't text and drive; don't play with matches; don't swim without adult supervision; don't litter; wear a seatbelt, etc.

4. With the paints, color in your phoenix. When it is dry, write a safety tip on each feather with the black marker.

5. Punch a hole in each wing, attach the string through the holes, and hang.

Druze

"Scooby-Doo, where are you?" Casey Kasem was the voice of Shaggy, friend and owner of the cartoon dog Scooby-Doo. He is also the host of numerous popular radio shows, such as *Casey's Countdown*. He is also a Druze. Some of the first Lebanese immigrants were members of the Druze community. The Druze are a religious group that incorporates aspects of Islam, Judaism, and Christianity, although they often worship as Muslims or Christians when living in those communities. They call themselves Ahl al-Tawhid (People of Unitarianism) or al-Muwahhidun (Unitarians, Monotheists) and were some of the first people to recognize equal rights for women. They also made slavery illegal, abolished discrimination, and were some of the first in the Eastern Hemisphere to practice equality.

Druze settled in small towns across the country, with the largest population in Seattle, Washington. Until recent times, they were very private about their religion, as they did not want to face discrimination. Almost 70,000 Druze live in the United States today. Most of the early Druze came to the United States from rural areas and had farming skills; Lebanese hills were dotted with their fruit orchards and olive groves. Their ancestors were experienced at growing olive trees, one of the oldest cultivated trees in the world. Some olive trees date back to Roman times and have enormous trunks. Not only are olives a delicious and healthy food, but their oil was sometimes associated with wealth. The olive branch is also an international symbol of peace. Early Lebanese immigrants brought the precious oil and olive oil soap to America.

Craft Olive Oil Soap

Soap making started in Greater Syria and was taken to Europe by the crusaders. Today, the world-famous Lebanese olive oil soap is said to cure dry skin, dandruff, hair loss, and skin diseases and to make skin glow.

It takes a long time to make and cure the prized olive soap from Lebanon, but you can try this short version.

What You Need

Adult supervision required

Covered work surface

Grater

4-ounce bar of plain, unscented
　　Castile soap

Cutting board

Double boiler with bottom ⅓ full
　　(you can make a double boiler
　　by stacking 2 pots together)

Stove

Spoon

1 tablespoon olive oil

Mold or small plastic container in
　　a shape you like

Plastic wrap

What You Do

1. Grate the soap onto the cutting board, being careful not to hurt your fingers.

2. Place the grated soap in the top of the double boiler and bring the water in the bottom to a boil. Lower the heat to a simmer and stir occasionally until the soap melts. Remove from the heat, let cool for a few minutes, then stir in the olive oil.

3. Pour the mixture into your mold and let it sit for 24 hours. Remove your new soap from the mold and wrap it in plastic until you use it.

Like other Lebanese Americans, the Druze have been an active part of American life for over 100 years and are very much in the public eye. The Alley family started the World Blindness Outreach, which organizes volunteer doctors to restore eyesight to poor people around the world. Salwa Roosevelt, President Reagan's chief of protocol, oversaw the diplomatic corps from 1982 to 1989, the longest anyone has served in that position. Writer Julie Maharem has taught at the American University of Beirut in Lebanon, served as president of the American Druze Society (the only woman to ever be elected to that position), and authors a website on the Druze people.

Dr. Gary Paul Nabhan (1952–)

Dr. Nabhan is called the father of the local food movement and believes that locally grown foods, raised without toxic chemicals, are healthier for the environment and people. Nabhan is an ecologist and ethnobotanist. An ethnobotanist studies the agricultural customs of different cultures. He is also an internationally acclaimed writer and sustainable agriculture activist. Sustainable agriculture means farming in a way that will help, not hurt, the earth so that crops can grow in the future, too. Dr. Nabhan has spoken out about the horrible effects that wars and bombing have on the environment. Several of his projects help preserve the ancient agricultural wisdom and plants of the Pima and other Indigenous peoples of the Southwest.

Grow the Famous Four

Mint, parsley, thyme, and basil are popular herbs used in Lebanese American cooking. Make a windowsill garden, decorating your pots with the Lebanese words for the herbs.

What You Need

Adult supervision required

Covered work surface

4 permanent markers, any colors that will show up on the pots

4 ceramic or terracotta flower pots with drainage holes and saucers, 6 to 12 inches deep

Pot of boiling water

Small mint, parsley, thyme, and basil plants

1 bag of soilless potting mix

Water for watering the plants

Edible fertilizer such as Grow More Organic Herb Food

Sunny windowsill that gets at least 5 hours of sun a day

What You Do

1. With the markers, write the Lebanese Arabic name of each plant on a pot:

   mint   نعناع   (nih-NAH)

   parsley   بقدونس   (bak-DOO-ness)

   thyme   زعتر   (ZAH-tar)

   basil   ريحان   (ree-HAHN)

   You can draw designs on the pot, too.

2. Put the pots in the sink and pour boiling water into each to sterilize them.

3. Remove the plants from the pots they came in and rest them on your covered work surface.

4. Put about 3 inches of potting mix in each pot. Add each plant to the pot with its name and fill in with potting mix until it will stand up. Gently tamp down the mix. Leave an inch of space at the top for watering.

5. Water lightly, as herbs don't like to be wet. Remember to check to see if your plants have enough water by sticking your finger about an inch down in the soil. If it's dry, add a little water. Place the pots on a sunny windowsill. Fertilize once a month, following the directions on the fertilizer bottle.

6. Once you see new growth, you can cut some herbs to use, taking care to always leave at least a third of the plant so it will grow back.

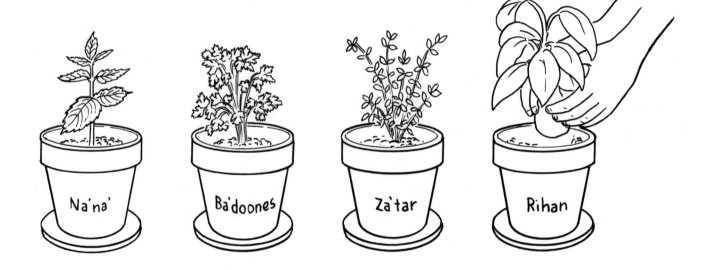

Danny Amos Jacobs Thomas (1912–1991)

Danny Thomas was a well-loved and popular entertainer. Born in Deerfield, Michigan, he did odd jobs to help his parents, who had nine children. Danny was drawn to the entertainment field, but after his first child was born, Danny prayed to St. Jude, the patron saint of the hopeless, asking for a sign: Should he stay in show business even though he wasn't making enough money to support his family? Danny promised to erect a shrine to St. Jude if the saint would guide him. Shortly after, his career took off. He became well known to American audiences for his starring role in the long-running, Emmy award–winning television show *Make Room for Daddy*. But Danny remembered his promise to St. Jude. The promised shrine he built was St. Jude's Hospital, a place where sick and needy children would be cared for regardless of race, religion, or ability to pay. Danny Thomas was active with the hospital until his death. His three children, including his famous daughter, Marlo Thomas, worked alongside their father. Today, St. Jude Children's Research Hospital in Memphis, Tennessee, is one of the most advanced centers for curing children's diseases. The Danny Thomas Memorial Pavilion on the hospital grounds features aspects of Lebanese culture as well as the life of Danny Thomas. Arched panels inscribed in Arabic and English describe both the founder and the hospital's mission:

"He who denies his heritage has no heritage."
"No child should die in the dawn of life."
"Those who work for the good are as those who do the good."

Not many Lebanese immigrated to the United States after 1924—America had closed its doors to people from the Middle East. Although their numbers were not large, a second wave of Lebanese immigration began in the late 1940s and continued through the early 1960s. Most were fleeing the wars in their home country. They were professionals or had started their American lives as students in American universities.

The third and largest wave of immigrants started in the 1970s. Their history is very different from the first immigrants from Lebanon. Most people came from southern Lebanon, which was devastated by the Israeli-Arab conflict. About 35,000 people from one town alone had to pull up roots. They settled in southeast Michigan, which has the highest concentration of Arab Americans in the country today. Around half a million Arab Americans, most of them originally from Lebanon, live in the area.

Across the United States, there are 3 million Lebanese Americans. The cities with the highest population are New York; Dearborn, Michigan; Los Angeles; Chicago; Houston; Detroit; San Diego; Jersey City, New Jersey; Boston; and Jacksonville, Florida. Some of the country's most recognizable celebrities and entertainers are Lebanese American, such as Salma Hayek, an Oscar-nominated actress who is the voice of Kitty Softpaws in the animated movie *Puss in Boots*. Although many people know that Salma Hayek is also a Mexican American, her father has Lebanese ancestry, and her first name comes from the Arabic root word meaning "safe." Tony Shalhoub, Emmy Award winner for the hit show *Monk*, was a featured actor in the movies *Spy Kids* and *Men in Black*.

Create a Jack Hanna Book of Animals in Arabic and English

Danny Thomas helped save children, and Jack Hanna helps saves animals! Conservationist Jack Hanna (1947–) grew up on a family farm and discovered his love for animals at a young age. In college, he got into trouble for keeping a donkey in a shed behind his dorm and ducks in his room. He turned his love for animals into a lifelong mission to save them, and his hard work led to dozens of conservation efforts all over the world. Today he is the host of *Wild Countdown* and other animal conservation shows. Make an animal book to share with ill children at St. Jude's or in your community. Use the English and Arabic words for animals. To make it even more interesting for kids, you can add the animals' names in other languages, too. Jazz up your animals by filling them in with patterns and colors in Helen Zughaib's style!

What You Need

Scissors

Poster board or lightweight cardboard

Glue

Gift wrap paper with small designs,
    preferably animals or comic strip paper

Scrap paper

Pencil

White printer or copier paper

Construction paper, any color

Colored markers or pencils

Pen

Hole punch

Yarn, any color

Ruler

What You Do

1. Make a cover by cutting out two pieces of poster board or cardboard, each 6 inches by 9 inches. Cover both with glue and gift wrap paper or comic strips. Set aside.

2. Draw your animals on scrap paper. Be sure not to make them larger than 4 inches by 6 inches.

3. When you are satisfied with your design, fold a few sheets of white copier paper in half. Draw an animal on either side of the fold. Decorate them with patterns or just color. Cut out each animal.

4. Make pages for the book by folding construction paper in half. Glue your animal pictures on each side. With the markers, write the name of each animal beneath it in Arabic and English.

5. Insert the pages between the book covers, lining them up so they are even. Punch two holes on the closed book edge, string the yarn through them, and tie it. Write the name of the book on the front cover.

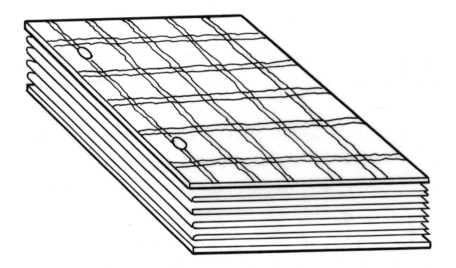

CAT: QITTA   DOG: KALB

40

6. Write a get-well note to go with the book and send.

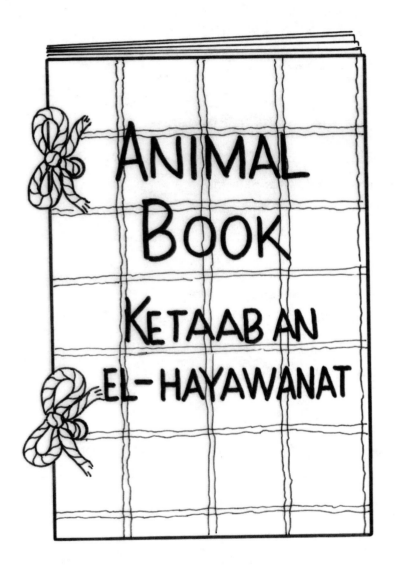

animal book		ketaab an el-hayawanat
camel	لمج	(JA-mal)
cat	طق	(kitt)
dog	بلك	(kalb)
elephant	ليف	(feel)
fish	ةكمس	(sa-ma-KAH)
giraffe	ةفارز	(za-RAH-fah)
kangaroo	رغنك	(kan-GAR)
lion	دسأ	(ah-SAD)
peacock	سووواط	(TAH-woos)
turkey	يمور كيد	(deek-ROO-me)
turtle	ةفاحفلس	(sul-HOE-fah)
rabbit	بنرأ	(ar-NAB)
zebra	شحولا رامح	(hi-MAR al-wah-SHE)

You can find more and hear pronunciation of the Arabic at www.softarabic.com/animal-names-in-arabic.

Lebanese Americans in Government and the Military

Victor Atiyeh (1923–)   First Arab American governor.

General George Alfred Joulwan (1939–)   Former Supreme Allied Commander in Europe, professor at West Point Military Academy.

Ray LaHood (1945–)   US Secretary of Transportation and former congressman from Illinois.

George Mitchell (1933–)   United States Senator from New Hampshire, 1989–1995.

Lt. Alfred Naifeh (1915–1942)   WWII Navy hero. Naifeh saved countless lives when his battle-ship, the *Meredith*, was sunk. He died as a result of his efforts, and the US Navy named a ship after him, the USS *Naifeh*.

Dr. Donna Shalala (1941–)   First Arab American to serve in a cabinet position. She was the first woman to be Secretary of Health and Human Services (1993–2001). She was awarded the Presidential Medal of Freedom, the highest honor given a civilian.

Lebanese Americans in Sports

Edward G. "Eddie" Elias (1928–1998)   Founder of the Professional Bowlers Association.

Doug Flutie (1962–)   Professional Hall of Fame quarter-back and founder of the Doug Flutie Jr. Foundation for Autism, an organization dedicated to helping families of autistic children.

Jennifer Shahade (1980–)   Two-time American Women's Chess Champion and founder of 9 Queens, an orga-nization that helps girls and at-risk youth benefit from the game of chess.

Fouad Zaban (Contemporary)   Football coach at Fordson High School in Dearborn, Michigan, and a star of the TV show *All-American Muslim*. His team is featured in the documentary *Fordson: Faith, Fasting, Football*.

Lebanese Americans in Literature

Elmaz Abinader (1954–)   Award-winning writer of *Children of the Roojme* and founder of Voices of Our Nations Arts Foundation.

Dr. Barbara Nimri Aziz (Contemporary)   Founder of the Radius of Arab American Writers and a writer and host of the Pacifica Radio show *Radio Tahrir*.

Dr. Philip Khuri Hitti (1886–1978)   Introduced the field of Arab culture studies to the United States. He was a Maronite, a scholar of Islam, and author of over a dozen books, including *The Syrians in America*.

Ameen Rihani (1876–1940)   Considered the father of Arab American literature, he was the first Arab American to publish a book in the United States, *The Book of Khalid*, in 1911.

Lebanese Americans in the Sciences

Dr. Elias James Corey (1928–)   Organic chemist who won the Nobel Prize in Chemistry in 1990.

Dr. Michael DeBakey (1908–2008)   One of the greatest heart surgeons in history. His invention made open-heart surgery possible, and he was one of the first scientists to link smoking with lung cancer.

Dr. Douglas Haddad (1976–)   A pioneer Internet radio host for a health, fitness, and lifestyle show called *The Dr. Doug Show*. He is an author, educator, nutritionist, public speaker, and avid musician.

• 3 •
Syrian Americans

Raheel dangled her bare feet in the cool creek. Her shoulders ached from her heavy pack, but at least her feet didn't hurt anymore. They had gotten hard and calloused from peddling her wares up and down country roads and city streets six days a week, but she liked it better than working in a factory, like some of the other Syrians who lived in Pennsylvania. In her well-stocked pack, she carried beautiful rosaries and vials of holy water from the Holy Land, her native Syria. She sold these religious items, made by Syrian villagers, along with her own handmade lace tablecloths and pillowcases. Ornate bottles of cologne, hairpins, combs, ribbons, and intricately carved wooden jewelry boxes were also part of her little traveling store.

Craft a Wood Inlay Box

The art of mosaic wood from Damascus, Syria, dates back several hundred years. Syrian mosaic is prized as the best in the world for its quality, accuracy, and beauty and is created in small family-owned workshops. Many Syrian American families consider them heirlooms. The beautiful trays, boxes, picture frames, furniture, and even clocks are imported from Syria.

You need lots of time and patience to make a mosaic wood piece. Different woods, such as peach, apricot, walnut, olive, and rose, are cut into long sticks.

Next, the artisan glues them onto the surface in geometric patterns of ovals, rectangles, squares, circles, parallelograms, triangles, heptagons, octagons, and so on. Even the making of the special traditional glue takes a long time. The artist then carves places for the teeny, perfectly cut mother-of-pearl pieces and sets them into their matching spaces—it's sort of like putting together a jigsaw puzzle with evenly shaped pieces. A layer of glue is applied to the entire surface, and then the mosaic is polished and sprayed with a coat of lacquer.

What You Need:

Adult supervision required

Covered work area

Unpainted flat-topped wooden or papier-mâché box

Brown acrylic paint

2 paintbrushes, one large and one small

¼-inch-wide painter's tape

Metallic pearly-white acrylic paint

Rose, orange, and red acrylic paint

Water for cleaning brushes

Clear varnish spray (optional)

What You Do

1. Paint the box brown and set it aside until it is dry.

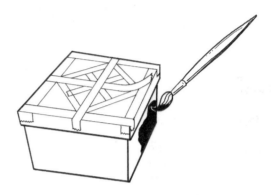

2. When the box is dry, make a grid using strips of tape to create any kind of geometric designs—squares, triangles, circles, ovals, etc.

3. Paint the individual designs in your choice of color. Let dry and remove tape. Spray with clear varnish spray and let dry.

Lonely farmwives always took time from their busy schedules to welcome Raheel, anxious for a glimpse into her wondrous backpack and for a glimpse of her. Most had never met a person from her country. They thought Raheel's bag was quite magical. It was an enormous valise when filled with her treasures, and when it was empty it could be folded into a small parcel. When Raheel went from door to door in towns, she usually worked alone, but out here in the country, she traveled with a few friends. The Pennsylvania farmland reminded her of Amar, her hometown nestled in Syria's rolling hills covered with olive trees. Raheel had come to the United States in 1896, two years earlier. As she sailed into New York Harbor, she had imagined herself on a grand adventure, much like the ones she had read about in *The Three Musketeers* back home in the missionary school. And like a true adventurer, she didn't mind the hardship of walking miles and miles with her heavy burden from one farmhouse to another in rain, snow, or blistering heat.

Raheel was proud that she could send some of her money home to help her family and to import new merchandise. And she saved some of her earnings so that she and Yusef could open a dry goods store in Allentown, Pennsylvania, after they married. Many people from Amar lived in Allentown, and although she missed her family, she enjoyed getting together with her Syrian friends, talking and playing the same games she had growing up in Syria.

Make and Play Mancala

Mancala comes from the Arabic word *naqala* (to move). It is the name of a group of board games now played in almost every country and sometimes referred to as "sowing" games, or "count-and-capture" games. Some historians believe that it is the oldest game in the world, and although no one really knows when and where it was actually invented, its roots are Arabic and African. In the ancient Syrian city of Aleppo, there is a centuries-old mancala game carved on a gigantic block of rock. The two facing ranks of six shallow pits have larger hollows scooped out at each end. The same design is carved on columns of the temple at Karnak in Egypt, and it appears in early tomb paintings in the valley of the Nile. Today mancala games are played widely in the United States, especially on the computer. Arab Muslims introduced chess to Europe centuries ago. As popular as mancala, chess is played in schools and tournaments across America. Syrian American Yasser Seirawan is a four-time United States chess Grandmaster champion, chess author, and commentator.

What You Need

Covered work surface

Cardboard egg carton with a flat top

Scissors

Acrylic paint in any color

Large paintbrushes

Tape or stapler

72 kernels of popcorn, small pebbles, jewels, pony beads,
   or small buttons that will be the playing pieces, or seeds

An opponent

What You Do

1. Separate the top of the egg carton from the bottom by cutting along the hinge. Cut off the front flap as well.

2. Cut the top of the carton in half, crosswise. These will be the end cups or storage bins.

3. Paint the insides of the three pieces any color(s) and let dry.

4. With the inside of the two halves of the top facing up, slide one underneath each end of the bottom, leaving them extending beyond the bottom by a couple of inches. Join the pieces together using the tape or staples.

Play the Game

1. Place the game board between you and your opponent with the larger cups on the right and left of the players. The six pits on the side of the board closest to each player, as well as the end bin on each player's right, belong to that player. The object of the game is to end your turn with no "seeds" in any of your pits except the end bins.

2. Put six seeds in each of the 12 pits.

3. The first player takes all the seeds from one of his six pits. He sows the seeds by putting one in each pit, moving counter-clockwise, including his own storage bin if he gets that far. If the last seed in his hand goes in his storage pit, he gets another turn. Otherwise, his turn ends.

   The second player repeats the "sowing" play. Players don't drop seeds in each other's storage pits.

4. If, during a turn, a player's last seed lands in one of his own empty pits and there are seeds in his opponent's pit immediately opposite it, the player gets to capture both his last seed and the seeds opposite. The opponent gets to keep any seeds remaining on his/her side. The seeds are counted and the player with the most wins.

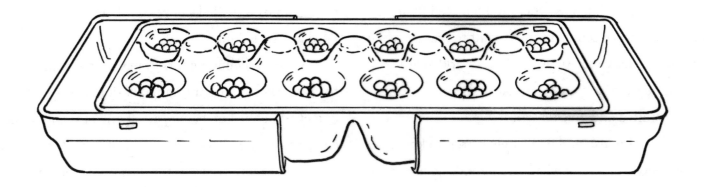

Raheel put on her shoes and stood up. She and her friends helped each other get the heavy packs back on their shoulders while they shared news of friends and family who worked in factories or owned stores in faraway places like Rhode Island and Texas. Raheel had never intended to stay in America. She had just planned to have her adventure, save money for her family, and return to Syria, but now Pennsylvania would be her forever home.

The story of how Raheel became an American is like the stories of so many others who came to the United States in the late 19th and early 20th centuries. Countless articles and books have been written about their bravery, determination, and creativity as peddlers. They would trudge into unknown territories laden with heavy burdens in the most horrible weather. Some did not survive, as they often did not have shelter. But most Syrians held other kinds of jobs. Worker-hungry American factories respected the strong work ethic of Middle Easterners and tempted them to immigrate. In fact, they paid scouts in the Levant to recruit people and show them how to move to America. After World War I broke out in 1914, new Syrian immigrants as well as other Arab Americans were recruited and quickly sent to fight on the frontlines. They spoke little English and had barely gotten to know the geography of their adopted county when they found themselves in the armed services and far away in foreign countries such as France and Germany.

Raheel came at a time when a map of the country of Syria looked very different than it does today. It was a large country in the Middle East, referred to as the Levant or Greater Syria. *Levant* is an English word borrowed from French which means "rising" or "the point where the sun rises." Considered the crossroads between East and West because it linked three continents, its boundaries were the Mediterranean Sea on the west, the Taurus Mountains on the north, the Arabian Desert on the south, and the Syrian Desert on the east. Damascus, Syria's capital, is said to be the oldest continuously inhabited city in the world, dating back to 9000 BCE. Today, Greater Syria is divided into five different countries: Lebanon, Syria, Jordan, Palestine, and Israel. Located on the eastern end of the Mediterranean Sea, it borders Turkey, Lebanon, Israel, Iraq, and Jordan on the south. It has mountain ranges, prairies (called steppes), a desert, and a volcanic area, the Jabal al-Druze Range.

Many early immigrants from Greater Syria left their country as Syrians, but their original nationality was changed if their hometown ended up being part of one of the new countries. To complicate matters, most were classified as Turks when entering the United States because the Turkish Ottoman Empire ruled

Syria at that time. In general, people from the Levant identified more with their region and religion than their country, much like people in the United States are proud to be Southerners or New Yorkers. Today most Americans who came from historic Greater Syria would be considered Lebanese, not Syrian. Syrians and Lebanese share a lot of similar stories, and some communities today are called Syrian Lebanese as they are home to both.

Have you ever felt like you were different from everyone in your school? The early Syrians really felt different compared to other immigrant groups. One reason was that there were not that many Syrians. They stood out and were not always treated well by Americans. Some Syrians anglicized their names, which means they changed their Arabic names to English names so they would fit in better. Some translated their first name into English and made it their last name. For instance, Yusuf is Arabic for the first name Joseph, and it was adapted for a last name. Then they often chose a completely new first name, usually a name from the Bible. So someone whose original name was Yusuf Youwakim may have come to be known as David Joseph. That way, they felt like they were still connected to their birth country, yet they didn't seem so different from other Americans. This was not just an Arab custom—many new Americans from many countries anglicized their names.

Like other people in the Levant area, Syrians were affected by many invasions and wars that had nothing to do with them. Many left Syria to save their families from poverty. During World War I, Syria was still occupied by the Ottoman Empire, which sided with the Germans. The country became a military base for the Ottomans, although the Syrians themselves were on the side of the British and the United States. But the Syrians suffered greatly, and many died of starvation because the Allied Forces would not allow food into Syria and the Turkish soldiers took all of their crops. After the war, the League of Nations gave the French control over the region. It was not until 1946 that Syria became an independent country.

Hundreds of years ago, many Arab cities had thriving silk workshops. Damascus, the capital of Syria, was known for its part in the silk trade. The city produced over 40 kinds of silk. In the more modern times of the 19th century, Syrian women cultivated silkworms in their own home businesses. Kids helped out, as the tiny critters eat and eat and must constantly be fed. As happened with the Lebanese, the Syrian livelihood of silk production was shattered when the mulberry trees, the main food of the silkworms, were destroyed by a disease. The silk industry dried up, but the Syrian passion for textiles did not. The early immigrants to America brought along their crosses, rosaries, and other items from the Holy Land to sell. But they also brought their love of beautiful fabrics and fashion and even put a multicultural twist into their designs, making everything from silk kimonos to fancy lace handkerchiefs. Along with Lebanese and other immigrants, they labored in textile plants from Paterson, New Jersey, to Lowell, Massachusetts.

Denise Hajjar (contemporary)

Fashion designer Denise Hajjar comes from a "fashionista" family. Her grandmother was a designer, and her grandfather owned a dress factory and was a patternmaker in the Middle East. Born and raised in Boston, Denise wanted to stay close to her Syrian roots and family. After graduating from college, she started her business in Boston and soon became world renowned as a top designer—her outfits are sold in stores across the nation. She creates costumes for movies, plays, and television. Vanna White on *Wheel of Fortune* has turned the letters while wearing Hajjar's gowns. Her clothes are worn by celebrities, politicians, and news anchors at events and award programs such as the Tonys, the Emmys, and the Oscars. Denise Hajjar has received the Lifetime Achievement Award in Fashion, the Vision Leader Award, the Exceptional Women Award, the Distinguished Alumni Award, and the Rising Star of the Year Award, as well as many others. Close to her heart is her work with St. Jude's Children's Hospital. Hajjar says, "Giving back should be the rule, not the exception." For her efforts in raising millions of dollars for St. Jude's, she and her committee received the Volunteer Group of the Year Award.

Design a Sarma Embroidered Scarf

Sarma is a type of embroidery done in Syria; *sarma* means "a wrapped thing" in the Turkish language. Because the Turkish Ottoman Empire occupied Syria, some Turkish words have become integrated with Syrian. Artists use gold thread and a satin stitch to fashion beautiful designs on cotton clothing, scarves, and tablecloths. Often the artist stuffs cotton behind the designs to give it a raised, 3-D look. Hundreds of years ago, embroiderers used real gold, rubies, and pearls to sew intricate designs on saddles, horse blankets, clothing, and household items. Some of these pieces can still be seen in museums. Today sarma artists use the technique on chic jackets and wedding gowns. Sarma has found its way into haute couture, or high fashion.

What You Need

Covered flat surface

Index cards or other light cardboard

Pencil with a sharp point

Ruler

Scissors

Plain cotton scarf

Gold fabric paint pen

4 gold bell tassels

Needle and gold thread

What You Do

1. Using the cardboard, make five or six templates in a diamond shape, 1 inch wide at the center point. Cut out.

2. Lay the scarf out flat.

3. Create a design in the center of the scarf by forming a flower with the diamond templates. Lightly trace the design with the pencil. Color it in with the gold fabric pen.

4. Make a rickrack line around all four edges of scarf with the gold fabric pen—you can add more than one line. Leave flat and set aside to dry.

5. When the paint is dry, sew a tassel in each corner of the scarf.

Christians

From 1875 to 1920, many Syrian immigrants were Christian, belonging to the Syrian Melkite Church. An Eastern Catholic Church, it is part of the worldwide Catholic Church. Melkites trace their origins to the early Christians of Antioch, Syria, and are located in Syrian Lebanese communities. Others belonged to the Syrian Orthodox Church, which is considered the most ancient Christian church. Orthodox churches across the country are divided into two archdioceses and have helped preserve the culture of Syrian Americans. Syrians also belong to a variety of Protestant groups. Some of the early people were also Jewish and Muslim.

Jews

Like other Syrian immigrants, many of the first Jews were peddlers and settled mainly on New York City's Lower East Side in the early 1900s. And like other Syrians, they were not always accepted by Euro-Americans. Even others of the Jewish faith, who referred to them as *Arabische Yidden*, or Arab Jews, were not always welcoming. The Syrians felt deeply insulted, as according to legend, the first synagogue in the world was built by King David in Aleppo, Syria. However, the Syrians supported each other. And when they were able, most of the community relocated to the Gravesend area of Brooklyn, New York, which today is the largest Syrian Jewish community in the world. Community members have thrived in the business world, still maintain tight relationships, and keep their traditions.

Druze

Many Druze who came to America in the early 1900s grew up on wheat farms in Syria. The Druze day of worship is Thursday, and they are in the habit of keeping their services secret to escape discrimination for their beliefs. The Druze have often avoided conflict when living in communities where they are the minority by practicing *taqiyya*. That means that one can join another tradition to keep safe, but still remain a Druze. They believe that many religions and ethnic groups can live together in harmony and equality and are known for their fairness, generosity, and hospitality. Today, they attend an annual convention held by the American Druze Society to stay in touch with others around the United States. The society has chapters in 16 states.

Muslims

The stinging winter winds howled around the first mosque in the United States as Muslims worshiped in their cozy underground room. Built in 1929, it was not in New York City or another urban area. The small, efficient building was right in the middle of the rugged prairie of Ross, North Dakota, and was built to withstand the elements. A new mosque was constructed on the same site in 2005, a testimony to the strength of the Syrian Lebanese Americans who first settled there in the 1900s. The oldest standing mosque, built in 1934, is in Cedar Rapids, Iowa. The State of Iowa has declared it a historical site. Its members came to the area as peddlers, opened stores, and served the local farmers. Some historians estimate that about 20 percent of the early Syrian immigrants were Muslim, but they often hid their religion to avoid persecution. Others converted to Christianity, at least in name, so they could feel part of their new home. The United States prided itself on being a place where people would be free of religious persecution, yet indigenous peoples, Jews, Muslims, and many different Christian sects had difficulty feeling accepted. Still, they settled in different places, such as Quincy, Massachusetts, and Michigan City, Indiana, and worked alongside other immigrants or opened stores.

Alawi

The Alawis are the largest minority group in Syria, but there are very few of them in the world. They identify as Muslims but have their own particular interpretation of Islam. Most Alawis live in a northwestern province of Syria called Latakia, which includes coastlines and rugged mountains. In 1900, Alawis began coming to the United States, and like other Syrians, they faced many challenges in their new country. Though they found themselves fighting in the armed forces, many did not even speak English. Although many left their new jobs to fight, others toiled in the factories. In New Castle, Pennsylvania, many Alawis, along with other Syrians, were employed in the tin mills. The men usually lived in boarding houses run by other Syrian immigrants until they could support a bride from the old country and buy a little house in the Syrian community. The modest two-story houses near the tin factories had comfortable front porches and small backyards with thriving gardens. These gardens helped feed people during the Great Depression of the early 1930s.

Today in Cleveland, Ohio, there is a very different garden filled with roses, trees, and history. This one honors Syrian Americans and is called the Syrian Cultural Garden. Nestled in an area that celebrates the diversity and peace among the people of the Ohio area, six granite pedestals are inscribed with the story of Syrian contributions to the United States. Emerging out of the gardens are Syrian-style arches, like the famous Palmyra Arch of Triumph, ruins from the desert Syrian city, Palmyra. The gardens celebrate the legacy of Cleveland's Syrian Americans.

New Castle, Pennsylvania

After several decades of living in New Castle, Pennsylvania, the Arab American community began to build their own places to worship and gather. In 1930 the Maronite Church of St. John the Baptist was founded, and in 1933 the St. Elias Syrian Orthodox Church was formed. The Alawis started the El-Fityet Alaween (the Alawi Youth), hosted many events and *heflas* (parties) for the entire Syrian community, and had a public space to worship instead of in their homes. The city has an Islamic center. The New Castle community is still strong, and today they celebrate at the annual Arab American Day. Syrians of all religious backgrounds are joined by representatives from other ethnic groups, civic leaders, and well-known business figures. Traditional food is served, Arabic dances are performed, and the riq and derbekke entertain the guests. Elders recount stories of racial discrimination they faced at local tin mills and factories before World War I.

Construct a Riq

The riq is a Syrian musical instrument that resembles a tambourine. It usually has a round wooden frame with a thin goatskin covering and cymbals. Both sides of the frame are covered with geometric inlay designs of mother-of-pearl or decorated apricot or lemon woods. There are five pairs of cymbals mounted in openings at even distances around the frame. The riq is played in a musical group called a *takht*, which consists of four main melodic instruments: oud, *nay*, *qanun*, and violin (or *jawzah*), and one main percussion instrument (riq). Sometimes there is a frame drum called a tabla or *daff*, too. Players do not sing. They usually play standing up as they move the riq up and down, shaking it hard while striking it like a drum. Learning the riq is difficult because one must learn to play all the different rhythms plus know the different tones that can be made by hitting the head.

What You Need

10- or 12-inch wooden embroidery hoop

Pencil

Strong packing tape

Permanent markers in black, pearl white, and silver

10 jingle bells

String

What You Do

1. Remove the outer hoop and set it aside.

2. With the pencil, make corresponding points on the inner hoop by marking a point at one side and another directly across from it. Repeat all around the hoop in 1-inch intervals. Have someone help hold the inner hoop and wrap the packing tape from one point on the hoop to the opposite point. Wrap around both points three times. Cut off the tape and press it down at the edges. Repeat this process right next

to the first point on the circle. Keep going until you have wrapped all the points on the hoop. Set it aside.

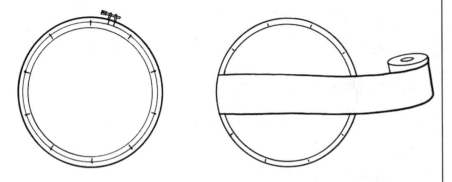

3. With the markers, make geometric designs along the outer edge of the outside hoop.

4. Slide each jingle onto a piece of string and tie it onto the outside hoop, evenly spacing the jingles all the way around. Put the smaller hoop inside the larger hoop, tighten the screw, and play!

The Syrians, whether Christian, Jewish, Muslim, or Druze, brought to America their love of family and family get-togethers. Like other Arabs, Native Americans, and some Asian and African cultures, they put more emphasis on the group than on the individual. Decisions were made that benefited everyone rather than just one person. Children were taught to visit older people and help in any way they could. At least once a week, long tables were set up for a communal feast of tasty dishes that were lovingly prepared and shared. Everyone helped. This tradition continues today in many communities.

Say It in Syrian

In English, the words for aunt, uncle, and cousins are the same whether the person is part of your mother's or your father's family. But in Arabic, the words are different depending on whether the aunt and uncle are the father's or the mother's relatives. The word for cousin is different depending on whether the cousin is male or female. If someone mentions his Aunt Mary, for instance, someone knows right away if Aunt Mary is the father's or mother's sister. Here are the Syrian words for a few family members.

Grandmother (your mom's mom)	TE-ta
Grandmother (your dad's mom)	JAD-dah
Grandfather (your mom's dad)	SE-do
Grandfather (your dad's dad)	JID-doh
Aunt (Mom's sister)	KHAL-ah
Aunt (Dad's sister)	Ahm-MA
Uncle (Mom's brother)	Khal
Uncle (Dad's brother)	Amm

Ice Cream Cones

You scream, I scream, we all scream for ice cream! Three people from Syria and one from Turkey all claimed to be inventors of the ice cream cone, including Ernest Hamwi, who is considered by most to have actually come up with the idea. At the 1904 World Fair in St. Louis, Missouri, he was selling *zalabia*, a crisp, waffle-like wafer popular in Syria. The ice cream vendor next to him ran out of clean dishes, so Mr. Hamwi rolled one of his warm wafers into a cone. When it cooled, the vendor put a scoop of ice cream in it and the ice cream cone was on its way to becoming America's favorite sweet! Today Hamwi is a very famous name in the pastry business.

Syrian meals are healthy, with several vegetables, whole grains, fruits, nuts, beans, and fragrant spices. Lots of lemons, onions, garlic, mint, and parsley are used to flavor foods. A typical Syrian meal begins with an assortment of *mezze* (appetizers) and a variety of nuts and pickles. The entrée features dishes made with meat, chicken, or fish, vegetables, salad, and rice, followed by coffee and tea, platters of fruit, and homemade pastries. A popular recipe and the national dish of Syria is *kibbeh*, a lamb or beef and bulgur wheat mixture. It can be eaten cooked or raw and prepared in a casserole or formed into little football shapes. Hummus has become a popular American food, available in stores throughout the nation, but the dish as we know it came from 18th-century Damascus.

Make Hummus

Hummus is the Arabic word for "chickpea," the main ingredient in this dish popular throughout the world. It's a healthy snack or appetizer and is usually served with pita bread.

What You Need

Adult supervision required

1 clove garlic

16-ounce can chickpeas or garbanzo beans

Blender or food processor

Measuring cup and spoons

¼ cup water

3 to 5 tablespoons lemon juice (to taste)

1½ tablespoons tahini (sesame paste)

½ teaspoon salt

1 teaspoon ground cumin

3 tablespoons olive oil

Serving bowl and spoon

Black olives and parsley for garnish (optional)

Pita bread cut into wedges, pita chips, or crackers

Makes 16 ounces

What You Do

1. Crush the garlic clove.

2. Drain and rinse the chickpeas.

3. Combine the garlic, chickpeas, water, lemon juice, tahini, salt, and cumin in a blender or food processor. Blend for 3 to 5 minutes on low, until thoroughly mixed and smooth. Drizzle one tablespoon olive oil into the blender as it is running.

4. Place the hummus in a serving bowl, and create a shallow well in the center of the hummus. Add the remaining olive oil to the well and garnish with parsley and olives.

5. Put a dollop of hummus on pita wedges or crackers and eat.

New Waves of Immigration

The second wave of Syrian immigrants came after World War II (1939–45) and included about an equal number of Christians and Muslims. Most of the first immigrants were poor and not very well educated, but the postwar new Americans were often well-educated professionals. A third wave started in the mid-1960s due to the Arab-Israeli conflicts in Syria. Over the next 40 years, almost 65,000 Syrians immigrated to the United States; 10 percent were admitted as refugees.

Many recent Syrian immigrants are medical doctors who came to complete their studies. The Syrian American Medical Society is known for providing quality medical services to needy patients. Dr. Abdul-Kader Fustock is a Houston-based plastic surgeon and the founder of Houston's chapter of the Arab American Medical Association. Dr. M. Zaher Sahloul is chairman of the Council of Islamic Organizations of Greater Chicago, serves on the national advisory board of the Catholic Theological Union, and is a physician at Advocate Christ Medical Center. Not only have Syrian Americans made important contributions to the health field, they have also been great inventors. Steve Jobs (1955–2011) developed, designed, and marketed the Apple line of products, pioneering the personal computing era.

Today Syrian Americans live in every state and they contribute in many ways to their neighborhoods and civic associations. The largest community is still based in the New York City metro area, with most living in Brooklyn. In early times, the center of the Syrian community was in lower Manhattan, which was also the hub of the national marketing network for both Lebanese and Syrians. The area was called Little Syria. Other urban areas, including Boston, Dearborn, New Orleans, Toledo, Cedar Rapids, and Houston have large Syrian American populations. Their cultural and social organizations can be found in several of these cities. They also settled in rural areas and are valued residents of smaller towns such as Utica, New York; Bethel, Connecticut; and Allentown and New Castle, Pennsylvania.

Judge Rosemary Barkett

¡Hola! Marhaba! Hello! The Honorable Judge Rosemary Barkett, born in Mexico to Syrian immigrants, is at home in Mexican and Syrian American cultures. Her family moved to Miami, Florida, when she was six; she grew up eating both Mexican and Syrian food and listening to conversations and music in Arabic, English, and Spanish. Not only is Judge Barkett comfortable in different communities, but she has had a variety of different careers, too. She always wanted to help people so instead of going to college right after high school, she joined the religious teaching order of the Sisters of Saint Joseph. Judge Barkett's parents were surprised—her mom wanted her to have children and her dad wasn't even Catholic. As Roman Catholic nun, she taught elementary and middle school. Judge Barkett attended college while still in the order, graduating with top honors. She then found a different way to help people. She left the convent to pursue a career in law, and again graduated at the top of her class from the University of Florida.

As practicing lawyer, Barkett began to rise through the judicial system. In 1985, she was appointed to the Florida Supreme Court making her the first woman, the first Hispanic American, and the first Arab American to ever serve in that position. Judge Barkett is active on and off the bench and is very involved in addressing the welfare of children, the criminal justice system, family law, and the role of women in the legal profession. She is known for her fairness and wisdom in making legal decisions. Eventually her abilities came to the attention of President Bill Clinton. In 1993 he appointed her to the US Court of Appeals, one of the highest courts in the country. Others recognize her wise counsel as well and Judge Barkett has received many prestigious awards such as the Judicial Achievement Award for her efforts in "protecting the rights of the individual." Two awards are given in her honor, including the Rosemary Barkett Award presented by the Academy of Florida Trial Lawyers to an individual who has demonstrated outstanding commitment to equal justice under law.

Judge Rosemary Barkett is grateful for her diverse experiences. She enjoys all of the Arabic and Mexican influences in her life, and she believes that embracing all cultures enriches our lives. Judge Barkett says, "Appreciation of peoples' identical hopes and dreams across all cultures will, I hope, lead eventually to acceptance of all peoples, including all of their differences."

Notable Syrian Americans

Paula Abdul (1962–)   Dancer, singer, and star of *American Idol* and *The X Factor*.

Sarab Al-Jijakli (contemporary)   Founding member of the New York chapter of the Network of Arab-American Professionals, an organization that encourages Arab Americans to help in their neighborhoods.

Audrey Cooper (1949–)   Director of the Multicultural Resource Center in Ithaca, New York, where kids can enjoy each other's cultural events, such as dragon boat racing and powwows.

Hala Basha-Gorani (1970–)   Anchor and correspondent for CNN's International Desk in Atlanta, Georgia.

Dr. Samuel Hazo (1928–)   First poet laureate of Pennsylvania and director of the International Poetry Forum.

Abraham Joseph (1923–2001)   A founder of the Sertoma Club, an organization that helps needy people with health issues, and a president of the Crippled Children's Society.

Alia Malek (1974–)   Civil rights lawyer, author of *A Country Called Amreeka*, and journalist.

Dr. Alixa Naff (contemporary)   Founder and consultant of the Smithsonian's Arab American collections and author of *Becoming American: The Early Arab Immigrant Experience*.

Jerome Allen "Jerry" Seinfeld (1954–)   Stand-up comedian, actor, writer, and television and film producer best known for the TV series *Seinfeld*.

George Shibley (1910–1989)   A California attorney who defended people that no one else would: his clients included labor organizers and minorities. In 1942, he defended 22 Mexican American youths in what came to be known as the Zoot Suit case, the largest mass trial in California history.

George Tanber (1951–)   An accomplished photojournalist who has covered the news in some of the most dangerous situations—from shark-infested waters to combat zones.

• 4 •

Palestinian and Jordanian Americans

The Statue of Liberty can spot the cars crossing the Brooklyn Bridge and steal a glimpse of a Yankee sliding into home base clear up in the Bronx. She keeps an eye on the Staten Island Ferry commuters and gives a shout out to the planes coming and going from JFK Airport in Queens. New York City is famous for its buildings, bridges, airports, and baseball teams, but down on the sidewalk, right in the heart of Manhattan, are SpongeBob SquarePants and Michael Jackson, painted by New York City's most famous sidewalk artist, Hani Shihada. His celebrated paintings have turned New York's sidewalks into open-air free art museums, illustrating walkways with some of the world's best-known people, books, and events.

Hani Shihada (contemporary)

Hani is a Palestinian American artist known for his New York City sidewalk art, but he didn't plan to trade his canvas for a pavement. Born to a large family in Jerusalem, Hani earned a scholarship to study at the Academy of Fine Art in Rome, Italy. He traveled on his own to faraway Rome, only to discover that the people who had promised him the scholarship had backed out. Should he return home or stay in Italy?

As he wandered around the great Italian city wondering what to do, Hani saw an artist drawing pictures on the sidewalk and was fascinated. He had always believed that art should be for everyone, and sidewalk art was available to all people, especially those who could not afford to buy it. It took art out of museums and brought it to the people. Soon his dismay at not having the finances to study was replaced by his passion for sidewalk art. Hani spent weeks observing Italian street artists, and soon he was drawing on the pavements himself.

Hani learned by observing others and by experimenting with chalk art on his own. Even among other sidewalk artists, he takes pride that his work is three-dimensional from all angles. He uses soft pastels and mixes his own colors. Hani rubs the pastel into the sidewalk to give the painting more strength and sprays a fixative when he is done. "It takes one to three days for one picture to be completed," he said. "There was one picture that took over a month and a half to finish."

After several years of teaching himself, he moved to Spain and then to the United States, where he became a citizen. He has been commissioned to do great "walks" of art by many different clients, including New York State, the Nickelodeon channel, and Disney. He's also painted huge murals that spruce up dull buildings around the country. Not only does he paint lots of imaginary characters, such as Beauty and the Beast and Super Mario Brothers, Hani is also known for his chalk portraits of some of the world's best-known people, such as United States Supreme Court Justice Sonia Sotomayor, who stopped by to have her photo taken with her sidewalk portrait. Beware of Hani's art—his 3-D pictures are so real you just might fall in!

Become a Sidewalk Artist

Sidewalk art is an Italian tradition that Hani and others brought to America. In 16th-century Italy, artists went from town to town sketching religious pictures on the pavement in village squares. The Madonna was a favorite subject, and these artists came to be known as Madonnari. Hani is not only an artist but also an educator, teaching entire classrooms how to make magic on sidewalks. He makes his own pastel chalk and describes it as like making dough for bread. He mixes up a bit of powdered pigments, chalk, soap, and hot water, and he kneads it until it's just right. Then he puts it in molds, and after it dries, the "paints" are ready to go. Hani tells young artists to build their art piece by piece. Start with an idea and just build on it until it grows bigger and bigger. He likes to do projects with kids that reflect diversity in people, nature, and objects. Hani says that seeing how the colors complement each other and live in harmony is a good way for us to create a more peaceful world. And all the colors stand up to the weather and wear, just like people!

What You Need

Permission to color on a safe pavement
  (e.g., sidewalk, driveway, playground)

Several friends

Rocks (optional)

Colored chalk

Paper towels

What You Do

1. Discuss a theme for your sidewalk mural, something that will give everyone a chance to work on a separate area and then combine it. Some ideas could be a playground, the kids in your class, or a nature scene, such as beneath the ocean surface. You are building a mural together, so talk over where the different pieces will go. If you are doing a nature scene, for instance, make sure the sky isn't divided by the water.

2. Divide the area into equal sections so that each artist will have an equal piece.

3. You can paint on rocks and blend them into your scene, but don't put them in areas where people may trip over them.

4. Start little and grow big. Use the paper towels to blend your work so it looks more realistic. When you are finished, sign your work and enjoy it until the next rain gives you a fresh "canvas"!

Palestine

Hani Shihada came to the United States much later than the first Palestinians, who came through Ellis Island. As most people from the Levant, they were not classified as Palestinian but as Turks or Syrians. Palestinian Americans make up part of the Palestinian Diaspora. *Diaspora* is from a Greek word that means "to scatter" and is a term associated with people who live in exile. Thousands of Palestinians were forced to leave their homes at the creation of the country of Israel, and many were never able to return. Today the land of historic Palestine has become an area that includes Israel, the West Bank, the Palestinian Territories, and the Gaza Strip.

From the late 1800s until the early 1900s, many Palestinians came to the United States, fleeing the Ottoman Empire that controlled their homelands. This was considered the first wave of immigrants, and most were Christians who quickly adapted to life in the United States. In the 1900s, more and more European immigrants began to settle in Palestine. They were facing religious persecution and genocide in their homelands, and in 1948 they formed the country of Israel. The fierce conflicts surrounding the creation of Israel displaced millions of Palestinians from their homelands despite the fact that they were in the majority. Several waves of Palestinian immigrants, both Christian and Muslim, came to the United States as refugees. Thousands more refugees came in 1967 after the Arab-Israeli War. In between and after the major wars in their homelands, Palestinians came to the United States from other Arab countries that had granted them refuge. It is hard to determine just how many Palestinian Americans there really are. According to the Census Bureau, about 200,000 people identify themselves as Palestinians in America. This is a much smaller number than the actual figure, because many were naturalized by other Arab countries, such as Syria, Lebanon, Jordan, and Egypt. Their documents state that those countries are their places of origin. Often Palestinians come to the United States to study but return to their adoptive countries.

Almost 3 million Palestinians were displaced from their homes during the 20th century, and a large percentage continues to live as refugees in various Arab countries. Some were naturalized by the countries that gave them sanctuary, but a great portion of them are treated as second-class citizens. Many live in horrible conditions without plumbing or proper homes. When possible, many Palestinians have chosen to move to the United States for educational and employment opportunities. Most Palestinian Americans live in Michigan, Florida, New York, New Jersey, New Mexico, and California.

People with Palestinian roots often long to go back to their ancestral homelands; many had houses that had belonged to their families for hundreds of years. Palestinian folklore, cuisine, culture, and arts keep Palestinians close to their traditions and preserve their heritage. Palestinian Americans celebrate weddings in the same way as other Americans, but with a special twist called the *zaffa*. A trumpet blows, announcing the zaffa, and the music transforms to Arabic with drum rolls, tambourines, and windpipe harmonies filling the air. A troupe of eleven people files in holding hands and performing a line-dance to the dabkeh beat. The men wear loose-fitting pants, head bandannas, and vests over striped shirts. The women are in long embroidered dresses and brightly colored embroidered headpieces. They all dance in unison. Once the line has moved to the center of the dance floor, more trumpet music is played, and the groom and bride enter the wedding reception.

The Art of Palestinian Embroidery, Al-Tatreez

Palestinian women's clothes are world renowned for their rich embroidery (*al-tatreez*) patterns and intense colors. The art played a significant role in the lives of the region's women. At one time, women in rural Palestine would gather to make their own clothes, pillowcases, tablecloths, and many other items by hand. But when their lives were turned upside down by their displacement from their homes in 1948 and then again in 1967, they could not afford the materials or the time to create their art. Today, some organizations have helped Palestinian women regain this centuries-old art form by providing embroidery materials to the refugee camps. Not only is this a chance to preserve the embroidery tradition, it also provides economic opportunities to families who can sell their art around the world.

Most often, the embroidery stitches show nature scenes or village life done in geometric forms. Some of the designs have funny names like "Old Man Upside Down" or "Chicken Feet." Other traditional stitches include "Moon of Bethlehem," "The Pretty Carnation," and "The Snake and the Serpent," to name just a few.

Embroider a Notebook Cover

Embroidery techniques take lots of time to learn. There are many different stitches from around the world and many different traditions of this ancient art form. Embroider your name with the basic split stitch and glue it onto a notebook cover.

What You Need

Notebook

Grip shelf liner, any color

Fine-point colored markers

Scissors

Ruler

Yarn in any colors except very light hues

2¼ yarn needle

Glue

1 yard of trim

What You Do

1. Measure the front cover of the notebook and cut a piece of shelf liner 2 inches smaller all the way around.

2. With markers, write your name or initials on the cut-out shelf liner. This will be the outline you will follow to make your embroidery.

3. Cut a piece of yarn 1 foot long and thread the needle. Tie a knot at one end—leave about 3 inches between the needle eye and the other end.

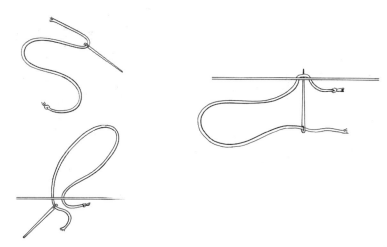

4. Start at the beginning of your outline by poking the threaded needle from the back to the front. Pull the yarn through until about 2 inches of yarn and knot are left on the back side. Move a half inch over on the outline and poke the needle through from top to bottom. Bring the needle back up through the middle of your stitch, splitting the yarn. (This is why it is called a split stitch.) Then put the needle back down through the shelf liner a half inch from where you went down the first time. Make sure you stay on your outline. Continue the split stich until your name is covered by yarn stitches. If you want, draw a few simple designs around your name and embroider them in the same way.

5. When you are finished, glue the shelf liner onto the notebook. Cut the trim to fit around the embroidery and glue it on.

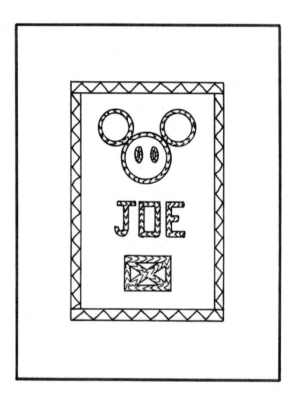

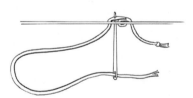

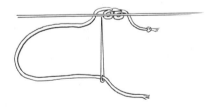

Naomi Shihab Nye (1952–)

At just seven years old, award-winning author Naomi Shihab Nye was already a published poet! She calls herself the "wandering poet," as she was born in Missouri, then lived in Palestine, then traveled all over the United States, and now lives in San Antonio, Texas, which she considers home. She has written over 30 books of poetry and novels, many of them, like *Sitti's Secrets*, for kids. In 2010, she was elected a chancellor of the Academy of American Poets. Naomi uses poetry to overcome stereotypes about Arabs and Arab Americans and often writes about her family, including her sitti (grandmother in Palestinian) who lived to be 106 years old! Not only is Naomi a famous author, she also works with organizations trying to create peace in the Middle East. One of her favorite projects is Neve Shalom/Wahat al-Salam (Oasis of Peace in Hebrew and Arabic), a village in Israel where Jews and Palestinians can work and raise their children together in equality and mutual respect. Today the community is home to more than 60 families, half Jewish and half Palestinian. Naomi writes about serious subjects such as peace, war, and the experiences of her dad, who was a refugee. But Naomi Shihab Nye also writes about everyday events and ordinary objects, helping the reader to see them in a different way.

Write a Poem Like Naomi Shihab Nye

Naomi Shihab Nye is a great observer of everything around her. She takes simple experiences and ordinary occurrences and turns them into magical treats for the reader. Naomi uses lots of imagery in her poetry. Imagery is when vivid and descriptive words are used to form mental images of things or events and appeal to one or more of the senses (sight, sound, touch, smell, taste). Instead of telling someone, imagery shows them like "the pitter-patter of rain against the window" or "the garbage smell punched me in the stomach." In the poem "Every Cat Has a Story," Naomi tells us what the cat thought of her violin playing and piano playing by saying it in a different way. Notice how many sensory images she uses in her poem.

EVERY CAT HAS A STORY
The yellow cat from the bakery
smelled like a cream puff.
She followed us home.
We buried our faces
in her sweet fur.
One cat hid her head
when I practiced violin.
But she came out for piano.
At night she played sonatas on my quilt.
One cat built a nest in my socks.
One inhabited the windowsill
staring mournfully up the street all day
while I was at school.
One cat pressed the radio dial,
heard a voice come out, and smiled.

Make a list of five animals or birds that you know or saw recently. Choose one from the list that pops out at you. Imagine that you have to tell a story about the animal without talking too much or using your hands to describe what happened. Try to think like the animal. What does your dog really think about when he sees you walk into the kitchen? How do robins know the right time to migrate south for the winter? Is there a head robin who tells them to pack up and go? Where does your hamster want to go when he tries to get out of the cage? By using colorful descriptive words in an unusual way, you can let the readers feel as if they are really there. Try to fill up your poem with as much feeling and emotion as you can.

Jordan

The Kingdom of Jordan borders the Mediterranean Sea, Israel, the Palestinian Territories, Syria, Iraq, and Saudi Arabia. Most of the area is hilly and mountainous. The country is rich in history and boasts many ancient ruins and sites, such as the brook where Jesus Christ was baptized and Petra, one of the world's most mysterious and ancient cities.

Queen Noor (contemporary)

Did you know that the Queen of Jordan was born in the United States? Arab American Lisa Najeeb Halaby became the first American-born queen of an Arab country, changing her name to Noor al-Hussein or "Light of Hussein." Queen Noor has been the first to do many things. She was in the first Princeton University class that enrolled women, cofounded the Jubilee School for gifted students in Jordan, established the Jerash Festival of Culture and Arts, formed the Arab Children's Congress, and founded the Women and Development Project to increase opportunities for women. Instead of leading the life of a fairytale queen, Queen Noor is active in humanitarian causes like Global Zero, an anti–nuclear weapons campaign, and she speaks up for world peace and the preservation of wildlife and natural resources.

Say It in Jordanian

Arabic is read from right to left, the opposite of English. Try learning to say these basic phrases in Jordanian.

Hello (mar-HA-bah)

My name is (ISS-me)

I don't speak Arabic (ma BAH-kee Arabi)

Many Jordanians are descended from the Bedouin, or as they are known in Arabic, the Bedu or "desert dwellers." These desert dwellers were experts in knowing where to set up their homes and how best to feed their herds in the harsh desert environment. Because the desert has a meager supply of plants and water, the Bedouin would stay in one place for just a short while and then relocate. That way, the limited plants and water were not destroyed and the natural resources could be replenished. They lived in harmony with their environment, giving the Earth a chance to live, too. Their ancestors chose this way of life, but today, most Bedouin live in cities or small communities and transport their animals by truck. However, they are still known throughout the Middle East for their great hospitality and kindness to strangers. One can always count on a good meal when visiting a Bedouin home. And Jordanian Americans are also known for their hospitality and tasty dishes.

Mix a Fatoosh Salad

What You Need

Adult supervision required

Oven

1 pita bread

Cookie sheet

1½ cups diced tomatoes

1½ cups diced, peeled cucumbers

¼ cup diced red onions

¼ cup chopped fresh mint leaves

½ teaspoon dried mint leaves

1 teaspoon sumac spice (If you can't find sumac, you can substitute ½ teaspoon apple cider vinegar and increase the salt by ¼ teaspoon.)

½ teaspoon salt, or to taste

2 tablespoons freshly squeezed lemon juice

¼ teaspoon ground black pepper

2 tablespoons olive oil

Medium bowl

Mixing spoon

Makes four 6-ounce servings

What You Do

1. Preheat oven to 375°F. Cut the pita bread into half-inch squares and arrange them on a cookie sheet in one layer. Bake for 4 minutes or until golden brown and crisp.

2. Mix all the ingredients in a medium bowl except for the toasted pita pieces.

3. Cover and refrigerate for 20 minutes.

4. Just before serving, add the toasted pita to the bowl and mix gently. Serve right away.

Compared to other groups, the number of people from Jordan living in the United States is small; they came later than other immigrants. Most arrived in the 1980s. About 60,000 Arab Americans identify Jordan as their country of origin. There are Jordanian cultural groups sprinkled across the country in cities like Washington, DC, and San Francisco, California. In many major metropolitan areas, entertainment aimed at Jordanians ranges from live stage presentations to radio and cable television shows. Some cable networks air Arabic movies, which is especially comforting to new immigrants and gives longer-term Jordanian Americans an opportunity to have a bit of the old country in America. Many Jordanian American gatherings feature music and dancing. The dabkeh is a dance that people of any age can enjoy, and about 20 types of the dabkeh are danced in Jordan! Arabs around the world compete to see who can get into the Guinness World Records for the longest dabkeh dance line. In August 2011, a group in the Lebanese village of Dhour Shweir set a new world record with a dabkeh chain of 5,050 people.

Create a Vest for the Dabkeh Line Dance

What You Need

1 yard of felt fabric in any plain color

Tape measure or ruler

Needle and thread

Fabric markers

Scissors

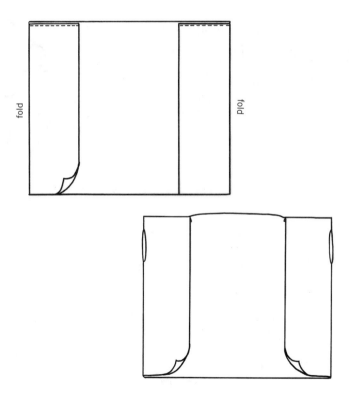

What You Do

1. Lay the fabric on a flat surface.

2. Measure 6 inches from the right and left sides of the fabric and fold each side in so that you have a 6-inch flap on each side. It will look like a tri-fold poster with the flaps closed. Sew the flaps along the top edge. Turn the fabric inside out so that the stitching is hidden.

3. Measure 2 inches from the sewn part along the fold and mark with a fabric marker. Measure 4 inches down from that mark and mark again with the fabric marker.

4. With the scissors, cut a slit along the fold between the two marks. Repeat on the other side. These will be the arm holes.

5. Use the scissors to round off the corners of the front flaps and decorate the vest with the fabric markers.

Notable Palestinian Americans

Ibtisam Barakat (contemporary)   Award-winning author of *Tasting the Sky: A Palestinian Childhood*.

Kamar Bitar (1964–)   A makeup and special effects artist for films including *The Adventures of Sharkboy and Lavagirl in 3-D*, *Spykids in 3-D: Game Over*, and *The Chronicles of Narnia: The Lion, The Witch and The Wardrobe*.

Dr. Joseph R. Haiek (1932–)   Founder of the Arab American Historical Foundation and Arab American Press Guild. In 2011 he was awarded the Ellis Island Medal of Honor.

Randa Jarrar (1978–)   Award-winning author of the young adult book *A Map of Home*.

Dean Obeidallah (contemporary)   A lawyer who became a comic as a way to address stereotypes and racism directed at Arab Americans. He is director of the Arab American Comedy Festival and cofounder of "Standup for Peace," a comedy show that fosters understanding between Arab and Jewish Americans.

Dr. Edward Wadie Saïd (1935–2003)   Professor at Columbia University and an advocate for Palestinian rights. He and Argentine-Israeli conductor Daniel Barenboim founded the West-Eastern Divan, a youth orchestra based in Sevilla, Spain, featuring musicians from Egypt, Iran, Israel, Lebanon, Jordan, Palestine, Syria, and Spain.

Farouk Shami (contemporary)   Created and owns Farouk Systems, a hair care and spa company. He also does hair design for many TV shows, including *The Apprentice*.

Maysoon Zayid (contemporary)   Actress, writer, and professional stand-up comedian. Her organization, Maysoon's Kids, provides scholarships and medical help for disabled and wounded refugee children and orphans.

Notable Jordanian Americans

Lily Bandak (contemporary)   The only Arab American photographer whose works are part of the White House's permanent collection. She is also Palestinian. She travels and works from her wheelchair helping others with disabilities through her foundation.

Steven Salaita (contemporary)   Professor at Virginia Tech and author of many books addressing Arab American issues and racism.

5

Egyptian Americans

The room was filled with guests—mothers, fathers, aunts, uncles, cousins, brothers, sisters, and friends. Suddenly the music started, and everyone got quiet. A woman in a long evening gown glided into the room with a tall, burning candle balanced in each hand. To protect her from the dripping wax, she held the candles in elaborately carved brass candelabras. She walked to the slow rhythm of the drumbeat. At times she swayed, her long billowing sleeves following the tempo. Then a group of teen girls dressed in beautiful party dresses appeared alongside teen boys in formal outfits. They stood in two lines. Each held a single tall candle with both hands. Their candleholders were not as elaborate, but the drip trays were wide enough to protect their young hands from the wax. Their candles were not yet lit. After the music stopped, the girls stood in a circle around the woman as she used her tall candles to light theirs.

Another woman crossed the threshold. She was not holding a candle, but in her arms was a chubby-cheeked baby sucking a pacifier. Dressed in a tiny white gown, he seemed happy to be there, although he was very little. The woman carrying the baby announced in a high-pitched voice that she wanted to introduce the baby to the world. This was the baby's Sebou, or naming ceremony. The Sebou is now part of the American landscape. There are so many Egyptian Americans in New Jersey that special businesses plan Sebou ceremonies much like a wedding planner plans weddings. They take care of the music, food, and logistics and ensure that the newborn babies and their families are very pleased by the naming event.

Baby showers in the United States are held to celebrate the coming birth of a baby, but Egyptian Americans celebrate when the baby is a week old and around to join in the fun. Of course, the baby is born in a hospital and given a name, but the Sebou ceremony is a chance for friends and family to get together to sing, dance, and take turns holding the baby and welcoming him or her to the community. The baby is taken on a tour of his or her new home. Grandparents whisper instructions to the baby and tell him to not listen to any others. Of course, they are just joking to add humor to the festive occasion. *Sebou* means "week"; a week is seven days, and seven is a very important number to Egyptians. The baby often gets seven of everything as gifts. Sebou bags that contain seven candies and coins are given out to guests.

Another celebration important to Egyptian Americans is the Sham Eniseem, which takes place the Monday after Easter. It literally means "smelling the fresh breeze" and is commemorated by Muslims, Copts, and all other Egyptians. A specially prepared fish dish, called *fiseekh*, is traditionally eaten on this day. Christians around the world dye Easter eggs, but Egyptian Americans, whether Muslim or Christian, decorate and color boiled eggs to celebrate the rebirth of spring. Most Sham Eniseem celebrations are held in parks and are happy outdoor events. In the United States, the Monday after Easter is not a holiday as it is in Egypt, so most Egyptian Americans choose to celebrate the occasion on Easter Sunday.

Many of the Egyptian celebrations observed today are believed to have started centuries ago. Ancient Egyptian civilization is perhaps one of the best-preserved old civilizations, and many aspects of it can still be seen in contemporary Egyptian life. The study of ancient Egypt provides a wealth of information that people love to study the world over.

What pops up when you think of Egypt? For most people it is images of the pyramids of Giza and the Sphinx. Egyptian American and Egyptian Egyptologists (archaeologists who specialize in archaeological sites in Egypt) have been at the forefront in the research while preserving the dig sites from damage. Dr. Alexander Badawy (1913–1986) was a well-known Egyptian American who taught Egyptology in the United States. He led several excavations in his native country, and his book, *A History of Egyptian Architecture*, is used as a reference book around the world. To make it possible for American archaeologists to study the ancient civilization, he funded a program at Johns Hopkins University where Egyptologists can pursue their studies.

Play a Game of Senet

Have you ever played backgammon? The great-grandparent of backgammon is senet, a board game first played in Egypt and now popular around the world. The earliest picture of senet appears in a wall painting in the tomb of the Third-Dynasty pharaoh Hesy, from about 2650 BCE. The tomb of the great queen Nefertari (1295–1255 BCE) displays a scene of her playing the game. Cecil B. DeMille's historic movie *The Ten Commandments* features a senet game between the queen and Moses called hounds and jackals. Since no records of rules have ever been found, there are many interpretations of how to play the game, and no one is really sure which interpretation is correct. The object of the game is to get each marker from square 1 through square 30 before your opponent does.

What You Need

Covered work area

Pencil

Ruler

20- by 6-inch (or larger) piece of heavy-duty cardboard

Black permanent marker

Colored markers

4 craft sticks for dice

Acrylic paints in blue, gold, black, and red

Paintbrushes

Water for cleaning brushes

10 bottle caps for pawns or playing pieces

What You Do

1. With the pencil and ruler, draw a grid on the cardboard. Make 3 rows of 10 squares, 2 by 2 inches each. Trace over the pencil lines with the black marker.

2. Start at the top left-hand corner and count to the 15th square, moving in a backward S. On the 15th square, draw the Ankh, the Egyptian hieroglyph for life. On square 26, draw three upside-down lollipops to represent the House of Happiness. On square 27, draw three wavy lines to represent

the House of Waters. On square 28, draw three dots to represent the House of Truth. On square 29, draw two vertical lines to represent the House of Re-Atoum. And on square 30, draw the sun symbol. You can color the symbols with the markers.

3. Paint the 4 craft sticks with different Egyptian designs, but only on one side. Leave one side blank.

4. Paint 5 bottle caps blue and the other 5 gold—these are the playing pieces or pawns.

Play the Game

1. At the beginning of the game, five pawns per player alternate along the first 10 squares at the top of the board—one blue, one gold, etc.

2. Throw the sticks to see how many moves each player gets. The first player to throw the sticks and get a 1 goes first (even if it's the first person to throw).
   - One patterned side up: player can move one space
   - Two patterned sides up: two spaces
   - Three patterned sides up: three spaces
   - Four patterned sides up: five spaces (there will never be a move of four spaces)
   - Four plain sides up: lose turn

3. When a pawn reaches a square already occupied by the opponent's pawn, they switch places. If your opponent has two or more pawns in a row, you cannot land on them and switch places. Players cannot land on their own pawn. You can jump over two pawns if you throw a 3 or 5, and you can't land on them with a throw of 1 or 2. It's good to land on an opponent.

4. If your opponent has three pawns in a row, you may not jump over and pass the three pawns, even if you throw a 5.

5. If you throw your sticks and can't move forward the number that you see on the sticks, then you have to move backward. If none of your pawns can move, either forward or backward, your turn is over. Only one pawn can be moved for each turn.

6. Some squares are safe squares and some are danger squares:
   - House of Happiness: all pawns stop here, no matter how many moves the player has
   - House of Waters: players who land here have to go back to the Ankh square
   - House of Truth: players who land here must throw a 3 to finish and leave the board
   - House of Re-Atoum: players who land here must throw a 2 to leave board

5. If a player has any pieces remaining in the top row, he or she cannot move any pieces off the board. The first player to get all pieces off the board wins.

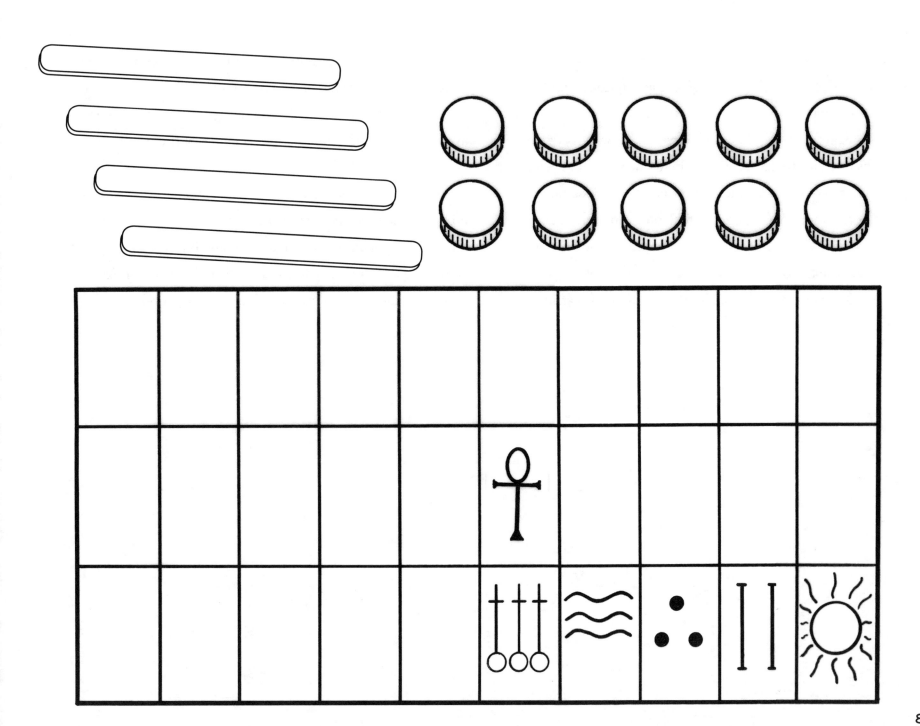

Egyptian hieroglyphics have fascinated people the world over. Hieroglyphics are the drawings and inscriptions found on the walls of the pyramids. The mystery of these words was unraveled when the Rosetta Stone, thousands of years old, was discovered and translated. In the 18th century, this stone was found in the Egyptian town of Rashid, which Europeans called Rosetta. The stone has two forms of Egyptian hieroglyphics and Greek carved into it. Because Greek is still a spoken language, scholars were able to translate the hieroglyphics, and the study of Egyptology was born. We learned a great deal about the pharaohs by learning to understand their language. But not only the symbols were interesting; so were the reliefs and paintings of people at festivals or participating in activities such as dancing and writing. The images gave modern people a glimpse into the lives of these early people and even their musical instruments. In some cases, the pictures documented the earliest use of instruments such as the reed flute and harp. The harp is the foundation for more modern instruments, including the piano. In fact, a piano is a type of harp that is positioned sideways inside a wooden body! Like other Egyptian inventions, the harp really traveled around the world.

Make a Harp

When we think of bagpipes or harps, we think of Ireland and Scotland. However, these instruments were traded to ancient people in the British Isles by the early Phoenicians, who traded items made in the Middle East to other parts of the world. Musical instruments attributed to the ancient Egyptians include drums, windpipes, and string instruments. Harps are considered the oldest stringed instruments. Hieroglyphics dating back 5,000 years show harps of various sizes. Some had 12 or 15 strings, while others had 19. They were played upright or upside down, with tuning keys at the bottom.

What You Need

Adult supervision required

3 chopsticks

Scotch tape

Yarn

Scissors

Hot-glue gun

Gold acrylic paint

Paintbrush

8 small rubber bands

What You Do

1. Form a triangle with the chopsticks, making sure the ends overlap. This is the harp frame. Tape the ends together.

2. Wrap yarn around each point of the triangle and glue the yarn in place with the hot glue. Let dry completely.

3. Paint the harp frame using the gold acrylic paint and wait for it to dry completely.

4. Slip the rubber bands one at a time over the frame. Place the bands so they run parallel to each other at equal intervals.

5. Glue the elastic bands where they touch the frame. Let the harp dry completely.

6. Pluck the harp to play.

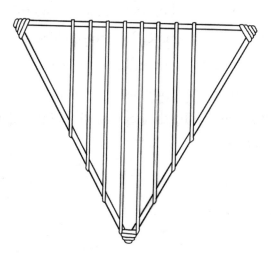

Halim El-Dabh (1921–)

Famous dancers Margot Fonteyn and Rudolf Nureyev have leaped across the stage to Halim El-Dabh's compositions. This celebrated Egyptian American musician has written, played, and composed music for over 70 years, adding a bit of Egyptian-inspired music to some of America's best-known orchestras and dance troupes. His primary instruments are the piano and the *darabukha*. Professor Halim El-Dabh has brought not only the mellow tones of Arabic music to American people, he has also introduced many different music styles from Africa and Latin America. Egyptian American soprano Christine Moore sang his music for his 90th birthday party at Lincoln Center in 2011.

Located in northeast Africa, Egypt is bordered by Israel to the northeast, the Red Sea to the east, the Sudan to the south, Libya to the west, and the Mediterranean Sea to the north. Ninety percent of the land is covered by desert. Ethnic groups include Nubians, Berbers, Bedouins, Arabs, Beja, and Dom. Traditionally, most people lived in harmony in Egypt and the majority of Egyptians who moved to new countries did so for economic or educational reasons. However, many Copts, Jews, and conservative Muslims left because they were concerned about the political climate in Egypt. Large-scale immigration did not begin until the 1960s; Egyptians are some of the most recent immigrants from Arab countries.

Initially, most of the immigrants from Egypt were Coptic Christians, a religious group founded in the city of Alexandria during the ninth century BCE. Coptic means Egyptian. When the ancient Roman Empire ruled Egypt, the Coptics were persecuted because they refused to worship the Roman emperor as a god.

When Coptic Christians immigrate to the United States, they can easily find churches and communities where Christianity is practiced. Today there are over 200 Coptic churches in 40 states from Alaska to Florida. Their domes make them recognizable— an organization of Egyptian American architects help design them. Some feature elaborate tile designs, another invention of ancient Egyptians.

Tile Art

The word *tile* comes from a French word, *tuile*, but the root word in Latin is *tegula*, or "roof tile of baked clay." In English, the word *tile* applies to any kind of flat clay applied to any surface. The history of tile production started over 4,000 years ago in Egypt, where they were used to decorate houses. Clay bricks were both sun baked and fire baked, and the first glazes were blue and made from copper. Colorful glazed tiles have been found in different pyramids and other ruins. Islamic artists perfected the manufacturing process and made tiles more decorative and intricate with geometric mosaic designs.

Tile art was used in Moorish Spain but did not spread to other parts of Europe until almost the 13th century. The methods used in the tile-making industry were closely guarded secrets passed down from fathers to sons. Improvement in tile production introduced firing kilns that hardened the tiles and made it possible to glaze them. Designs were often painted beneath the glaze, but soon the glazes themselves added to the artistic value of the tile. Advances in the field continue to this day.

Nawal Motawi (1964–)

You've heard of garage bands? Well, Nawal Motawi started her career as a garage artist! She was inspired by the tile craft of ancient civilizations as well as the American Arts and Crafts movement, so she set up a workshop in a garage to craft Christmas tree ornaments and sold them at the local farmer's market. In 1992, one of Motawi's customers hired her to design and create a fireplace, and it ended up being so spectacular that the word spread. Soon after, she moved to a bigger studio in Ann Arbor, Michigan, and her business grew. Motawi Tileworks has become a highly successful business that produces beautiful and functional masterpieces.

Motawi's tiles are known for their rich glazes and designs that are mostly inspired by nature and architecture. Though influenced by Arabic techniques, Motawi's tiles have uniquely American designs. Not only do the stunning tiles grace floors and fireplaces in private homes, but they adorn public libraries, parks, and other public spaces, too.

Design a Ceramic Tile Hot Plate

What You Need

Covered work area

Unglazed tile in any size

Ceramic paints in blue, green, yellow, orange, and red

Paintbrushes

Water to clean brushes

Shellac or transparent tile glaze

Felt

Scissors

Glue

What You Do

1. Paint a curved green line across the tile about one third of the way up, from edge to edge. This will be the outline of some desert hills or dunes. Paint the hills green and yellow.

2. Paint a red half circle over the curved line and below the top of the tile. This will be the sun. Paint the sun red.

3. Paint the area above the hills and around the sun blue.

4. Paint alternating lines of orange and yellow from the half-circle sun. These will be the sun's rays.

5. Let dry completely and then gently glaze the tile with the transparent glaze. When dry, cut and glue a piece of felt to the back of your tile so it won't scratch the table surface.

After air travel became possible, Egyptian Muslims began to immigrate to the United States. Air travel was key, because most practicing Muslims need to travel to Mecca in Saudi Arabia and perform the hajj pilgrimage. There are five pillars in Islam—each pillar is a duty that Muslim people carry out as a pledge to their religion. The hajj is the fifth pillar, and it requires every able-bodied Muslim to travel to Mecca at least once in his or her lifetime. Because the ability to fly halfway around the world would now allow them to keep their commitment to their faith, Egyptian Muslims were able to move to the United States. Another responsibility that all Muslims have is to observe Ramadan, the month when people renew their commitment to practice patience, charity, spirituality, humility, and submissiveness to God. Egyptian Americans observe Ramadan in much the same way as they do in Egypt.

Dahlia Mogahed (1974–)

Dahlia Mogahed helps the world understand Islam and coauthored the book *Who Speaks for Islam?* For six years, she researched and interviewed more than 50,000 Muslims in more than 35 predominantly Muslim nations. It was the biggest study ever done on Muslim people. President Obama appointed her to the White House Office of Faith-Based and Neighborhood Partnerships.

The Nile River

The Nile is the longest river in the world. Over 4,000 miles long, it runs through 10 countries in Africa before flowing into the Mediterranean Sea. Since Egypt is mainly desert, the land along the Nile was a source of both food and transportation for Ancient Egypt, as it is today. Most Egyptian communities are located near it. It is usually considered a disaster when a river floods, but this is not the case for the Nile. Ancient civilizations depended on the annual summer flood to deposit silt onto the riverbanks. This black silt was what gave the river one of its Ancient Egyptian names, Ar, which means "black." Another name given to the river is Iteru, meaning "great river." Most of the cultural and historic sites of Ancient Egypt are found along this great waterway.

Travel in ancient and modern Egypt includes a variety of boats. The Nile has always been a great way to move and to transport goods and equipment from one part of Egypt to another. Before electricity and batteries, candles were used to light the paths of all those who set sail on the Nile. The boats glimmered with lights from lanterns made of brass and glass, called fanouses. These traditional lights are still used in Ramadan celebrations today, much like candles are used in Buddhist, Hindu, Jewish, and Christian rituals. People fast during the day and come out after dark—the fanouses light their way as they visit one another's homes. Children carry their fanouses in the streets and sing special Ramadan songs to celebrate the holy month.

Light a Fanous Lantern

Fanous lanterns traditionally made in Egypt are shaped from brass with geometric patterns drilled into the metal. Some craftsmen weld metal shapes around tinted glass, while others insert glass slabs within the metal frame. Fanous makers set up shop in Khan El-Khalili, a marketplace so old and famous that no visit to Egypt is ever complete without seeing it. It is not unusual to find sixth- and seventh-generation fanous-making craftsmen, and they take great pride in their work. Most fanouses that are handled by children are plastic and battery operated. Traditionally, candles were used to light the lanterns.

What You Need

Adult supervision required

Covered work area

Clean, clear plastic jar at least 4 inches wide, with a lid—
   try to find a many-sided jar like the one fancy jams come in

Ruler

Hammer and nail

Acrylic paints in any colors, including gold

Paintbrushes

Water for cleaning brushes

Gold or silver glitter

1 foot of gold cording

Tissue paper, any bright color

Permanent markers, any colors, including black

Glue

Scissors

Toilet paper or paper towel roll

Flat-bottomed plastic gems

Battery-operated tea light

What You Do

1. Remove the jar lid and use the hammer and nail to punch two holes about 2 inches apart in the middle of it. Paint the lid gold and cover it with glitter. Set it aside to dry.

2. When the lid is dry, thread the cording through the holes and tie the ends together in a knot. This will be the fanous handle.

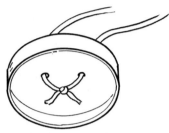

3. Cut the tissue paper into small pieces. Mix equal parts white glue and water and apply it to the inside of the jar, where the tissue paper will go. You can follow the designs on the jar or make your own design. Adhere the tissue paper to the glue and then put another coat of glue over the tissue paper.

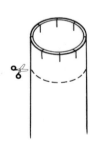

4. Paint designs on the outside of the jar with markers or paint. Outline your tissue-paper design with black markers.

5. Glue on the gems in a pattern of your choice.

6. Cut a 1-inch piece off the toilet paper roll. Make eight ½-inch slits around the edge of the roll and bend the pieces outward into tabs. Put a dab of glue on each tab and press it onto the inside of the jar bottom. This is your tea light holder.

7. Turn on your tea light and put it in the holder at the bottom of the jar. Screw on the lid and enjoy your lantern!

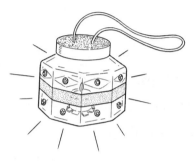

In 1970 a dam was built along the Nile that stopped the flooding. This changed how farming was done in Egypt, but the water from the river is still used to grow a variety of crops like wheat and broad beans, called *ful* (fava beans). Fava beans, an Egyptian staple, are used to make falafel. Falafel means "little bite" and is called *ta'miyyah* in Egypt. The deep-fried patty is often made with chickpeas in the United States. It was first invented in Alexandria, Egypt, some say by the Coptic people as a replacement for meat during Lent. Since Alexandria is a port, sailors from all over took the delicious little patties home, and eventually falafel became a popular fast food all over the Middle East and now around the world.

Cook Egyptian Falafel

What You Need

Adult supervision required

Covered work area

15.5-ounce can fava beans
  or chickpeas

Colander

Food processor

1 tablespoon flour

2 green onions

1 clove garlic

½ cup chopped parsley

½ cup chopped cilantro

1 teaspoon ground cumin

1 teaspoon paprika

¼ teaspoon cayenne pepper

1 teaspoon salt

¼ teaspoon pepper

½ teaspoon baking soda

Small ice cream scoop

⅓ cup flour in a small bowl

Large frying pan

Enough corn oil to fill the
  frying pan 2 inches deep

4 pieces of pita bread

Salad of lettuce and diced
  tomatoes

Makes 4 sandwiches

What You Do

1. Drain and rinse the beans well in the colander.

2. Place the beans, onions, garlic, spices, and baking soda in the food processor and pulse until completely mixed and finely chopped.

3. With the ice cream scoop, scoop up ping-pong-size balls of raw falafel. Flatten the falafel gently between your palms to form a patty.

4. Roll the patty in dry flour in the small bowl to remove excess moisture and prevent splattering.

5. Fry the patties in corn oil over medium-high heat. When the patties turn brown, flip them. It takes about 20 seconds for each side to brown.

6. Fill each pita with at least two falafels and some salad. Add tahini dressing.

We often hear the term *Egyptian cotton*. It is yet another famous Egyptian crop nourished by the Nile waters. The word *cotton* is derived from the Arabic word *kotn*. Cotton is made into clothing, towels, and bedsheets. Egyptian cotton used to be very expensive, but thanks to advances in technology, items made of Egyptian cotton have become more affordable. The prized cotton has longer fibers than other cottons, making items soft, luxurious, highly absorbent, and long lasting. Today, different kinds of cotton are grown in Egypt, but the best quality is grown in the Lower Egypt area. Fabrics made with this Lower Egyptian cotton never look frayed or shabby, even after years of use. Varieties of Egyptian cotton are also grown in the United States. Evidence of similar types of this useful plant has been found in archaeological sites in the United States dating back several thousand years. Today the United States is the world's top exporter of cotton. Pima cotton, for which the United States is known, was formerly called American-Egyptian cotton. Its new name was given in honor of the Pima Native Americans who grew the cotton in Arizona starting in 1910.

The Littlest Lamb Orphanage

Attorney Mira Riad's family owns a luxury-textile company. She grew up in a wealthy suburb of New York City, far away from poor neighborhoods. But she felt drawn to helping the less privileged, especially orphaned children in Egypt. Riad started the Littlest Lamb Organization, which built and supports a home for orphaned children near Cairo, Egypt. Kids live in the family-style orphanage until they are ready to go to college, which is paid for by the organization. Although she has never had children or celebrated their Sebou, Mira Riad is a mom to hundreds of kids, her "little lambs."

Sew a Kaftan

A kaftan, which is a floor-length robe usually made of cotton, is often loose fitting and well suited to Egypt's warm weather. Its flowing, free design allows air to circulate around the body, which, along with the cotton material, makes for very cooling articles of clothing. Kaftans are worn by both men and women and are slipped over the head. Women often embroider the top part of their kaftans, while men generally wear them plain or decorated with vertical stripes.

What You Need

Adult supervision required

60-inch square white tablecloth in any fabric

6 safety pins

Tape measure

Pinking shears

Fabric marker

Fabric glue

Rickrack in various lengths and colors

2 yards ribbon, any color

What You Do

1. Fold the tablecloth in half and place it on a tabletop with the opening at the bottom. Use four of the safety pins to pin both sides together so it does not unfold

2. Put a dot right in the center of the folded edge. Measure 5 inches from that dot to one side and make another dot. Do the same from the center dot to the other side. You will have three dots. Cut along the fold from one dot to the other. This will be the opening for your head.

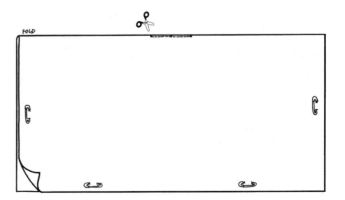

3. Measure 5 inches from the fold down each side and pin. This will be your sleeve.

4. Using fabric glue, draw a line on each side from beneath the safety pin marking the sleeve area to the opening at the bottom. These will be your side seams. Press the seams together with your fingers so the fabric bonds.

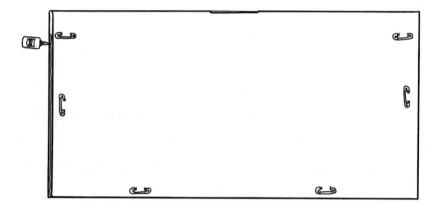

5. Decorate your kaftan with rickrack in patterns of your choice. Remove the safety pins and slip the kaftan over your head like a T-shirt. If you want a sash, tie the ribbon around your waist.

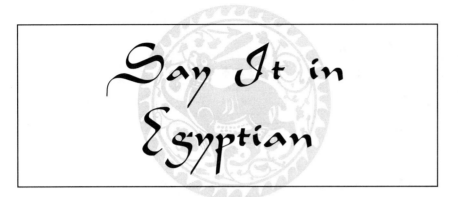

Say It in Egyptian

Most Egyptian Americans are from Egyptian cities where people wear Western-style clothing. Some Egyptian fashion and jewelry designers have been inspired by the high fashions of Europe, and many Americans have worn fashions designed by Egyptian American Issac Mizrahi. In rural areas, women are known for wearing bangles and elaborate necklaces to enhance their outfits. Ornately decorated cuff bracelets that were worn by both men and women in the time of the pharaohs remain popular even today.

Egyptian Americans bring their language to the United States as well as their ceremonies and recipes. They speak Arabic with a special Egyptian lilt. Most Egyptian dialects are similar, although some areas have been influenced by the Nubian language. Egyptian Arabic pronunciation is much softer than classical Arabic. In many ways, Egyptian dialect among Arab languages is similar in tone to the Italian language among European languages. During Ramadan, children sing a song about a sultan's daughter dressed in a kaftan. You can make your own tune or just say the beautiful poem. It sounds nice in English, too.

Ramadan has come (Wahawi ya wahawi. Ee yo ha.) (the chorus
    that is repeated throughout)
The sultan's daughter (Bin til sultan. Ee yo ha.)
Is clad in a kaftan (Labsa Oftan. Ee yo ha.)
Ramadan has come (Wahawi ya wahawi. Ee yo ha.)

Make a Cuff Bracelet

Cuff bracelets are usually made of silver, gold, or copper and decorated with inscriptions and gems. Today many Egyptian artisans are still inspired by designs from the time of the pharaohs. Design your own cuff bracelet. You can make one for each arm.

What You Need

Covered work area

Ruler

Pencil

Empty toilet paper roll

Scissors

White glue

1 piece of heavy-duty foil, 8 inches by 10 inches

Plastic gems and small rocks in various colors

What You Do

1. Using the ruler and the pencil, draw a straight line from one end of the toilet paper roll to the other and cut along the line to open it.

2. Cover the toilet paper roll with glue and press the aluminum foil onto it, smoothing it out as you go.

3. Fold the excess foil into the curved part of the toilet roll, gluing the edges to secure them in place.

4. Glue the stones along the foil in a pattern of your choice. Wait for the glue to dry and slip on the bracelet.

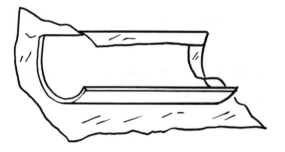

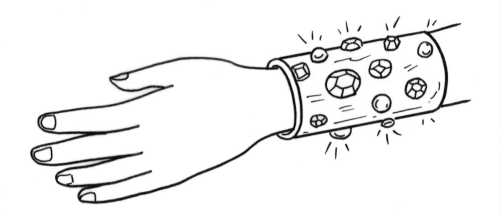

Stormwind is in terrible trouble! The city defends itself against the orcs in the video game *Warcraft: Orcs & Humans*. This first of real-time strategy games was developed by Egyptian American Allen Adham, and the technology changed video gaming forever. And speaking of "real time," have you heard of a femtosecond? It is one quadrillionth of a second, and in 1999, Ahmad Zewail won the Nobel Prize in Chemistry for his pioneering work in the field of femtochemistry, making him the first Egyptian American to win the prestigious award. The *Apollo* astronauts radioed from the moon, "Tell the king we're bringing him something from that little crater." They were referring to NASA

Who's on TV?

Egyptian Americans grace the airwaves from the movie screen to your living room television. Hoda Kotb cohosts the NBC *Today* show and works as a correspondent on NBC's *Dateline*. Laugh it up with Asaad Kelada, who directed funny shows like *Sabrina the Teenage Witch* and *Sister Sister*. Actress Wendie Malick is in *Alvin and the Chipmunks* and *Wild Horse Annie*. Rami Said Malek plays Pharaoh Ahkmenrah in the *Night at the Museum* movies and Benjamin in *The Twilight Saga: Breaking Dawn*. On a serious note, award-winning film maker Jehane Noujaim directed *Mokattam*, an Arabic film about a garbage-collecting village near Cairo. Suzy Kassem is a director and writer for kids' films, most notably *Harmony Parker*.

scientist Dr. Farouk El-Baz, who chose the landing site on the moon. Egyptian Americans can be found working as scientists and inventors in many different areas.

An estimated 800,000 to 2 million Americans can claim Egyptian heritage. The largest concentrations live in New Jersey, New York, California, Illinois, Florida, and Texas. Egyptian American kids play games at the King Tut Festival held by the Saint Antonius Coptic Orthodox Church in Hayward, California, and compete in the Girls Table Tennis Tournament at the Worcester Islamic Center in Massachusetts. Many aspire to become writers like award-winning journalist Mona Eltahawy, who stands up for women's rights, or professor Pauline Kaldas, who teaches writing. Egyptian American Sam Khalifa was shortstop for the Pittsburgh Pirates from 1982 to 1986, making him the first Arab American Muslim to play in the major leagues. From coast to coast and from Sebou ceremonies to school soccer teams, Egyptian Americans are part of American communities.

6
Iraqi Americans

Baseball and *bamia* (okra), violins and *jawzah* (a traditional Arabic instrument), cross country / track and grape leaves, Islam and Christianity, and jazz and *maqam* (traditional Iraqi songs) were all part of childhood for Iraqi American musicians Dena and Amir ElSaffar. Their father was born in Baghdad, Iraq, and their mother is a Euro-American. The brother and sister grew up in Oak Park, Illinois, a suburb of Chicago famous for its architecture, literature, and visual and performance arts.

Dena and Amir attended a Lutheran school where the children were mainly of German descent. Most of the time they were comfortable with their classmates, but they always felt different. Sometimes their friends said the ElSaffars had weird names, except of course, for their mother, Ruth. The focus in school was on European culture or Euro-American contributions to the world. During the rare times when lessons centered on Middle Eastern cultures, the information was not presented as enthusiastically as European history. Still, Dena and Amir loved learning about the glorious cultures of ancient Mesopotamia, which is now known as Iraq. Their dad had taught them that Mesopotamia was once a hub of culture and education. They enjoyed studying the life of Jesus Christ, who was born in and grew up in the Middle East. Such lessons gave them a link to the Arab world, where some of their relatives still lived. In class, Dena would flip through the pages of the Bible, looking for pictures of Jerusalem and Damascus. She knew the date palm desert scenes were similar to the landscapes where her father grew up, and it made her feel as if she belonged to a special place. Their father's homeland was the birthplace of many inventions, including some of the games still played today.

Play El-Quirkat

The modern day game of checkers came from the game of el-quirkat or *alquerque*. This earliest board game, dating back to 3000 BCE, was discovered in the ruins of Ur, an Iraqi city. The game boards are carved into the roof of the great temple in Kurna, Egypt. Moors took the game to Spain, and then it spread throughout Europe. The object of the game is similar to that of checkers—you try to capture your opponent's playing pieces.

What You Need

White poster board or cardboard, 8 inches by 11 inches

Ruler

Pencil

3 medium-point markers, green, red, black

Water bottle cap

Scrap cardboard

Scissors

2 players

Flat surface

What You Do

1. The el-quirkat board is a grid of triangles and squares. The 8-by-11-inch poster board will be the game board. With the ruler and pencil, measure and draw five vertical lines, 8 inches long and 2 inches apart. Measure and draw five horizontal lines, 8 inches long and 2 inches apart. Draw a border around the outer edge. Write A on the top left corner, B on the top right corner, C on the bottom right corner, and D on the bottom left corner.

2. With the ruler and pencil, draw a line from A to C and another from B to D. Mark the middle line between A and C with the letter E. Mark the middle line between B and C with the letter F. Mark the middle line between C and D with the letter G. Mark the middle line between D and A with the letter H. Draw a straight line between each of the following: E and F; F and G; G and H; H and E. With the ruler as a guide, go over all of the lines with the black marker.

And now give yourself a hand, as you have begun to learn geometry, a field of math introduced to the world by Arabs.

3. Use the bottle cap to trace 24 circles on the scrap cardboard. With the red marker, color 12 circles red; with the green marker, color 12 green. Cut out each circle.

Play the Game

1. Flip a coin to see who goes first.

2. Each player fills the first two rows at his end of the board with his pieces. The remaining two pieces go in the third row, to his right. There will be one free space in the middle of the board.

3. Pieces can be moved in any direction along the black lines to any free space. You capture your opponent's pieces by jumping them. If a player has a chance to jump and does not, the opponent gets to capture his piece.

4. The player who captures all his opponent's pieces wins.

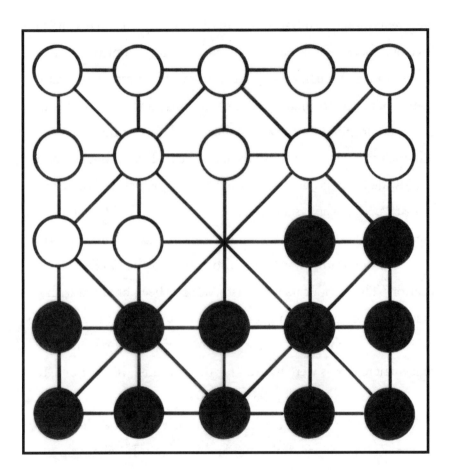

Dena and Amir's school had an amazing music program where Dena excelled on the violin and viola and Amir mastered the trumpet and ukulele. Their father introduced them to American jazz greats along with traditional Iraqi music. Their mom shared her love of American folk music. The gifted siblings continued their music studies through college and became world-renowned musicians, influenced by many music styles. After a visit to Baghdad, they were inspired to study Iraqi music and bring it home to America through melody, rhythm, and beat. Today, they perform worldwide in their own band called Safaafir, which is Arabic for "whistles." Their songs are a rich mix of centuries-old Iraqi melodies with a twist on modern American and classic European styles.

Did you know that Iraq is also known as the cradle of civilization? Throughout its long history, it has been credited with many firsts, including being one of the first places on Earth where humans lived, the place where the wheel was first used, and the place where words were written for the first time. It was home to the world's first cities and the area where fire was first used.

Modern Iraq shares borders with Turkey, Iran, the Gulf of Oman, Kuwait, Saudi Arabia, Jordan, and Syria. It is made up of four main regions: the desert west of the Euphrates; Upper Mesopotamia, between the upper Tigris and Euphrates Rivers; the northern highlands of Iraqi Kurdistan; and Lower Mesopotamia, the alluvial plain caused by flooding that extends to the Persian Gulf.

But ancient Iraq, or Mesopotamia, looked very different on a map than it does today. Mesopotamia, located between the Tigris and Euphrates Rivers, was spread over a vast area that includes present-day Iraq, Turkey, Syria, and Iran. Since then, Iraq has had more than just its name changed. It has been ruled by different foreign empires, the latest being Great Britain, which controlled Iraq until the 1930s. Even after Iraq gained its independence, it was still invaded when other countries felt their interests were being threatened.

Maqam

Maqam is a centuries-old vocal tradition of Iraq performed mostly in cities. Iraqi American musicians like the ElSaffars brought it to America. It combines musical styles from diverse Iraqi cultures, including Bedouins, rural Arabs, Kurds, and Turkmen as well as neighboring Persians, Turks, and others. Although the word *maqam* refers to a type of music used in the Arab world, the Iraqi maqam means the songs themselves. A maqam is a poem set to music and features the singer as the main performer.

Design a Birthday Copper Pendant

Historians say that the people of Iraq were some of the first to use copper. An ancient copper pendant was discovered in the area, and archaeologists using special dating techniques determined that it was made around 8700 BCE, almost 11,000 years ago! For thousands of years, Mesopotamian scribes used cuneiform, the first form of writing, to record daily events, trade, astronomy, and literature on clay tablets. Cuneiform numbers used a combination of just two signs: a vertical wedge for 1 and a corner wedge for 10. Using cuneiform, write your birth date on a pendant. For numbers not listed, combine two cuneiform symbols. For instance, the birthday November 21 would have ‹⊤ for the 11th month and ≪⊤ for the 21st day.

What You Need

Covered work surface

2 matching flat wooden shapes, 1 to 3 inches

Copper acrylic craft paint (or make your own by mixing orange and burnt sienna)

Paintbrush

Water for cleaning brush

Pencil

Paper

Black fine-point permanent marker

Cording for necklace

Scissors

Glue

What You Do

1. Paint the wooden shapes on one side and let them dry. Flip them over, paint the other sides, and set them aside until dry.

2. Practice writing your birthday on the paper with cuneiform numbers.

3. When you are satisfied, use the black marker to write your birth date on the copper pendant.

4. Cut the cording to the size you want, making sure it can slip over your head easily.

5. Glue the cording onto the back side of the pendant. Glue the second shape on top so the cording is sandwiched between the two pendants. Put a heavy object on top and let the glue dry.

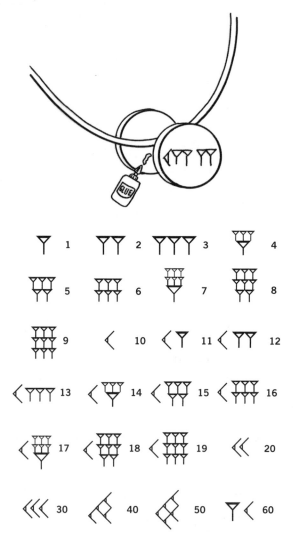

The oldest map in the world was discovered in Iraq in 1930. It was inscribed on a clay tablet and is thousands of years old. Ancient Iraq, also called the Land of Two Rivers, had an advanced agricultural system and thrived as a trade center. It was also a place where people of diverse backgrounds lived together in peace and harmony. Iraqi Americans reflect Iraq's diversity and can trace their ancestry to many different religions and ethnicities, including Islam, Judaism, Christianity, Arabic, Kurdish, Chaldean, Assyrian, Yezidi, and Mandean.

Chaldeans

The first people to migrate from Iraq to the United States were the Chaldeans, a religious and ethnic minority. They began to arrive in the United States around 1890, but the largest wave came in 1910 and settled mainly in the Detroit, Michigan, area. Attracted by jobs in the auto industry, Chaldeans also felt at home in Detroit because of the Lebanese Christian community. Their main religion was Catholicism; most belonged to the Chaldean Catholic Church as they do today. Although many of the early immigrants also spoke Arabic because they had lived in an Arab country, their primary language was Aramaic, the language spoken by Jesus Christ.

Over 95 percent of Chaldeans in the Detroit metro area can trace their origin to Telkaif, a Christian town in the northern Iraqi province of Mosul. Because of poverty, Chaldeans began leaving to seek economic opportunities and first relocated to nearby Iraqi cities and other places in the Middle East. Later, Chaldean men began to come to the United States; women and children remained behind until the men could provide for their families. The first Chaldeans put down roots and then encouraged others to come. This was called "chain migration" and was practiced by immigrant groups from around the world. Immigration from Iraq to the United States, as with all other Arab countries, all but stopped between 1924 and the 1950s.

Today the descendants of the first Chaldean immigrants work in a variety of areas. Many are professionals and are much better off economically than their parents and grandparents from rural Iraq. The early Chaldean Americans made sure their children took advantage of the educational opportunities they did not have in their home country. They are known for their entrepreneurial spirit; many own their own businesses and provide jobs for people in their communities as well as other Americans.

The most recent Chaldean immigrants, beginning in the 1990s, have come from the urban centers of Iraq and are better educated than the first immigrants. Many are refugees of the wars in Iraq. The Chaldean Federation, an American organization, resettles thousands of displaced people and helps them adjust to life in the United States. American Chaldean groups and churches have helped resettle Iraqi children in the United States who have been orphaned by war.

Baoutha

Chaldeans celebrate Baoutha (baa-oo-tha), which in Aramaic means "pleading." According to tradition, the Chaldeans in the ancient city of Nineveh—modern-day Mosul, Iraq—were suffering from a great famine. They asked God for help. Jonah was sent to aid them, but he did not do as God instructed and was swallowed by a giant fish. After three days and after Jonah asked God for forgiveness, the fish threw him up near Nineveh. Jonah finally delivered God's message: the people must repent for their bad actions and begin living in a good way or their city would be destroyed. Jonah was rewarded when each and every person gave up his or her wicked ways; no other prophet had ever been this successful. The king declared a three-day fast, and Jonah lived a very long and happy life. Today, Chaldeans fast three days before the beginning of Lent to give thanks for the miracle. Children often fast, too, so they can learn self-discipline. If people must eat, they eat light meals of vegetables and salads and stay away from meat and all animal products.

Make Bandora (Tomato Salad)

Bandora (BAN-DO-ra) is often eaten as part of a Chaldean meal. The tomato, which was developed by indigenous people of the Americas, is now very popular in Middle Eastern dishes. Middle Easterners borrowed and shared ingredients from different parts of the world and are credited with writing the world's first cookbooks. Clay tablets with recipes carved on them have been found in ancient Iraqi ruins, and many are over 10,000 years old! Like other immigrants, Iraqi people brought their tasty cuisine to the United States, adding to the richness of the American dinner table.

What You Need

Adult supervision required

Covered work area

Cutting board

Knife

2 large, firm tomatoes

1 medium onion

2 Kirby cucumbers or 1 large cucumber,

    washed but not peeled

Bowl

Juice from 1 large lemon, about 2 tablespoons

¼ cup olive oil

Salt and pepper

Makes four 6-ounce servings

What You Do

1. Cut the tomatoes, onions, and cucumber into small pieces.
2. Place the pieces in the bowl and add the lemon juice, olive oil, and salt and pepper to taste.
3. Lightly mix until the vegetables are coated with the lemon juice and olive oil. Serve right away.

Babylonian Jews

The second sizable Iraqi group to relocate to the United States practice Judaism. They migrated from Baghdad to New York City in the early 1900s seeking educational and economic opportunities like other Iraqi immigrants. Several more came after World War II began. Today, around 15,000 Iraqi Americans trace their ancestry to what is known as Babylonian Jewry, with the largest concentrations in California, Florida, and the Northeastern states. Jack Marshall tells the story of his family in *Baghdad to Brooklyn: Growing up in a Jewish-Arabic Family in Midcentury America*.

Newroz

According to Kurdish legend, almost 3,000 years ago there lived a horrible monster named King Zuhak. He was a giant with a serpent growing out of each shoulder, and he ate the brains of small children. Zuhak was so evil that the sun stopped shining and spring could not return. Crops withered and died. Birds and animals left. The land was cold and dark all the time. The people were scared and sad as every year more and more of their children were sacrificed to the evil king.

A courageous blacksmith, Kawa, tricked the king by giving him sheep brains to spare the life of his 17th, and last, child. He fled with her and hundreds of other children to the furthest and highest Zagros Mountains, where they could live in safety. Over the years, the children learned how to survive and feel peace and joy. Kawa taught them to defend themselves and turned them into a mighty army. The army marched on the kingdom, and men and women left their fields to join them. They stormed the king's castle, and Kawa killed King Zuhak. The sun returned, crops grew, and people were happy again. Today, Newroz is celebrated every March 21 to welcome back spring.

Little Kurdistan

Nashville is the country music capital of the United States, and it's also the home of Little Kurdistan. This Kurdish Muslim community of around 11,000 people, mostly from Iraq, is home to the world's largest population of Kurds outside Kurdistan! The first Kurds relocated to the area in 1978, after Nashville was designated as a relocation city for refugees. As a result of the Iraqi wars, refugees have been streaming into Nashville since 1991. Christian organizations sponsored and welcomed the Kurds, whose Muslim values are the same as those of the city's Christian groups. Both practice lifestyles that are family centered.

The Kurds are a non-Arabic people with a distinctive language and culture. Most belong to the Sunni Muslim faith and come from the mountainous area that includes parts of Armenia, Iran, Iraq, Syria, and Turkey. Kurds identify largely with their culture rather than that of any particular country. Today in Nashville, they celebrate the ancient holiday of Newroz, the Kurdish New Year, with dancing, singing, and a huge picnic that thousands attend.

Mad'an

The Mad'an people of Southern Iraq are also called Marsh Arabs; most are members of the Muslim Shi'a faith. They are descendants

Count in Kurdish

One	Yek
Two	Duh
Three	See
Four	Chwar
Five	Penjah

of one of the oldest cultures in the world. Many Biblical scholars say this is the area where the Garden of Eden was located. The Tigris and the Euphrates Rivers divide into hundreds of creeks and channels before flowing into the Persian Gulf, forming an area of vast wetlands larger than the Florida Everglades. For centuries the Mad'an lived in harmony with their extraordinary environment. Many of their homes sat on tiny islands built of reeds.

When the British ruled Iraq, they began to drain the marshlands to make more farmland, and this harmed the culture and environment of the Ma'dan. Then, 20 years ago, the area was almost destroyed when it was drained by the Iraqi government to punish the Mad'an for challenging the government of Saddam Hussein. Thousands were killed, and many more fled to nearby Iran, the United States, and other countries that gave them refugee status.

Millions of birds used to nest in the area or use it as a refueling stop while migrating between Africa and Siberia. Ornithologists (scientists who study birds) often used these remarkable areas to learn about these birds and identify new bird species. The 15-foot-high reeds and an abundance of fish provided shelter and food for a variety of species, many on the endangered list, but the pollution and draining of the marshes made it almost impossible for the birds to live there. Many people, like Dr. Azzam Alwash of the Nature Iraq project, are working to reverse the damage that was done to this area. One sign that the environment is being restored is that thousands of birds are finally returning to the marshes.

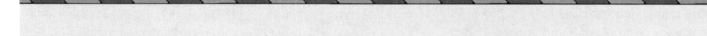

Nature Iraq

Nature Iraq was created by Iraqi American Dr. Azzam Alwash, a civil engineer determined to protect, restore, and preserve Iraq's natural environment and the rich cultural heritage that it nourishes. He grew up in Iraq and then came to the United States for his education and made it his home. Now he has returned to Iraq to help restore the marshlands for the Mad'an people. Dr. Alwash is helping bring back the native plants along with animals like lions, water buffalo, and otters. His plans include the development of the Mesopotamian Marshlands National Park, a preservation to protect wildlife. Nature Iraq involves indigenous Iraqis at all levels and promotes respect for traditional knowledge.

Create a Birdbath with an Arabesque Design

The Qur'an (the Muslim holy book) contains many references to the beauty of the natural world. Using interconnected, repeating geometric designs inspired by trees, flowers, and fruits, artists have been decorating walls, pottery, and tiles with an art form called arabesque (or *zakhrafa*, in Arabic) for centuries. The designs resemble a kaleidoscope picture. In honor of Dr. Alwash and his undertaking to save the birds of the marshlands, make a birdbath to give your neighborhood birds a treat. Maybe the birds who visit will be on their way to or from the Iraqi marshlands! You can also make a birdfeeder with the same instructions.

What You Need

Adult supervision required

Covered work surface

Well-ventilated area

1 terra-cotta pot, at least 8 inches in diameter

1 terra-cotta pot saucer, 20 inches in diameter

Flexible cardboard to make templates

Pencil

Scissors

Terra-cotta marker, any bright color

Acrylic paint pens in any colors except brown

What You Do

1. Wash the pot and saucer and let them dry completely.
2. Make two different size templates—one larger than the other—by tracing two different round objects, like a saucer or a bowl, onto the cardboard. The larger circle has to be at least 2 inches smaller than the terra-cotta saucer so you can trace around it. Cut out these two circles. Position the larger

circle in the middle of the saucer and trace around it with the terra-cotta marker. Make at least six other circles with the smaller circle template, making sure they interconnect in the first circle. Use the smaller circle for the pot and use the same technique to make flowers all around it. Make sure the flowers are evenly spaced from the top to the bottom. This will be a bit tricky, as the pot is not a flat surface.

3. Put the flowerpot upside down on the ground. Fill the saucer with water and place it on top. Do not permanently attach the saucer to the pot; it will need to be easily carried to a water source.

4. Do not leave the birdbath out in freezing weather, as it may crack. Remember to add clean water every day so birds can have a fresh drink and a bath.

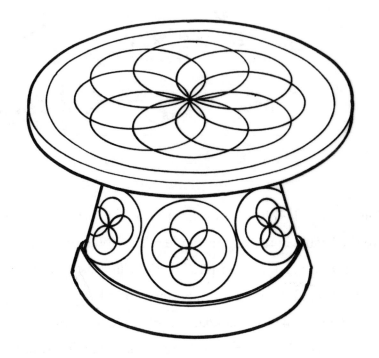

Yezidi

The Yezidi are a unique ethnic group with a religion, language, and culture distinct from the Arab and Kurdish cultures, among whom they live in northern Iraq. Their culture dates back to ancient Mesopotamia, and they have suffered discrimination in many countries for their religious beliefs. Many had to flee war-torn Iraq, but they have found sanctuary in Lincoln, Nebraska, designated by the United States as a resettlement city.

Mandeans

Still another minority group affected by the Iraqi war is the Mandeans, followers of an ancient religion, older than Christianity, Islam, or Judaism. They do not believe in war or carrying weapons. They must be near a natural body of water to conduct their ceremonies. A small group, they are facing extinction as a result of the wars. But a Mandean American doctor and Boston resident, Dr. Wisam Breegi, rallied for a number of them to be given refugee status and relocated to Worcester, Massachusetts, which now has the largest population of Mandeans in the United States.

Hard Times Adjusting to Life in the United States

The recent Iraqi immigrants face a harder time adjusting to life in the United States than the small number who settled in America during the 1960s and 1970s. Most of those immigrants had been educated in Western universities and were not casualties of war like the immigrants of the 1990s. They had been more thoroughly exposed to Western culture and had an easier time adapting. The refugee immigrants of the 1990s often found that the laws of their new American towns were unlike the laws of their home villages. American teenagers had more independence than Iraqi kids, and the focus was not on extended family but on school, sports, or jobs. Because the United States was at war with their home country, many Iraqis experienced prejudice from Americans just because of their nationality. It has been painful for Iraqis to see images of their villages and countryside being bombed on the nightly news. Many feel that the wars in Iraq have hurt too many Iraqis and Americans and wish for a peaceful outcome. Like other Arab Americans, Iraqi Americans have served their country in all branches of the United States military.

Today, the cities with the largest Iraqi American populations are Detroit, Chicago, San Diego, Nashville, Atlanta, and Phoenix. It is difficult to know just how many Iraqis call America home, but the estimate is 600,000 Iraqi Americans, most of them of Chaldean ancestry.

Iraqi American Women

From the Atlantic to the Pacific and from saving lives to writing poetry, Iraqi American women have been recognized in many areas for their leadership and contributions to the world. Zainab Salbi founded Women for Women International, a grassroots humanitarian organization that helps women survivors of wars rebuild their lives. Salbi has been honored by President Clinton and named the *Harper's Bazaar* 21st Century Heroine. Emmy award–winning journalist and filmmaker Anisa Mehdi has produced programs for PBS and National Geographic. Anna Georges Eshoo is a member of the US House of Representatives from California and is dedicated to clean energy and the environment. Dr. Dahlia Wasfi is an internationally known peace activist who speaks out against the Iraqi war. Halla Ayla's award-winning art presents the rich cultures of the Arab world. Dunya Mikhail was presented with the United Nations Human Rights Award for Freedom of Writing and was the first Iraqi woman to publish a poetry book in the United States.

Salah ad-Din Yusuf Al Ayoubi (circa 1138–1193)

One of the most beloved and respected leaders of all time was Salah ad-Din Yusuf Al Ayoubi, or Saladin, as he is sometimes called. He was Kurdish, and he won the hearts of all peoples in his empire, which incorporated most of Kurdistan, Syria, Egypt, and Yemen. He recaptured Jerusalem and other occupied Arab territories from the invading European crusaders in 1187. Salah ad-Din united Middle Easterners of all backgrounds and ruled with compassion and fairness. Even his military foe King Richard the Lionheart admired his chivalry, fairness, and courage. On one occasion, King Richard was not seen outside his residence for several days, so Salah ad-Din checked on him and found out he had fallen ill. He put aside his differences with King Richard and visited him with get-well tidings. Salah ad-Din was held in esteem in Europe as well as the Middle East; his name is familiar to students of medieval history. A brilliant military strategist, Salah ad-Din's ranks were well trained and ordered to spare lives whenever possible. When his soldiers entered the city of Jerusalem, they were not allowed to kill civilians, rob people, or damage the city.

Iraqi's current flag is black, white, red, and green. Green is said to have been the favorite color of the prophet Muhammad, and the black, white, and red represent banners of the medieval Islamic dynasties. There has been much discussion about designing a new flag that would also include Kurdish symbols.

Red	أحمر	(ah-MAR)
Black	أسود	(as-WAD)
Green	أخضر	(akh-DAR)
White	أبيض	(ab-YAD)

Notable Iraqi Americans

Dr. Hisham N. Ashkouri (1948–) Award-winning international architect of several projects, including New York City's "Playground for All Children," the first park for both able-bodied and disabled children. His designs set the standards for the US Post Offices.

Joseph Kassab (1952–) Executive director of the Chaldean Federation of America (CFA). He spearheaded Operation-R4 (Research, Relief, Resettlement, and Re-empowerment) to aid Iraqi refugees.

Dr. Yona Sabar (1938–) Professor and author who wrote *The Folk Literature of the Kurdistani Jews: An Anthology.*

Acrassicauda Iraq's first heavy metal band; the Chaldean group's four members now live and perform in the United States.

Tommy Hanna (1985–) Known as Timz, his award-winning raps tell of the suffering of Iraqis under the war occupation.

Justin Meram (1988–) First Iraqi American professional soccer player, he plays for the Columbus Crew major league soccer team.

Remy Munasifi (1980–) A rapper, comedian, and video artist who became a YouTube star under the name GoRemy.

7
Yemeni Americans

Sal walked into the house and hung his straw hat on the nail by the door. It had been a long day working in the California fields, 9,000 miles away from his Yemeni homelands. He could tell by the shifting winds that the new season was fast approaching. Sal knew he would have to go back out to milk the cows, but for now he would rest. He felt he had earned it today. A whiff of coffee brewing in the kitchen brought him to the present. Ahh, the smell of home. He preferred the stronger coffee of his native land, but he had gotten used to the sweeter tastes of California brands.

In 1900, Sal had arrived by boat in New York City, with only six dollars and the address of a relative. Fortunately, his cousin was good to him and had given him $200. "It's for coffee," he had said. Sal chuckled at that now. It was the perfect expression to make him feel that he was indeed talking with a relative. He had come from the place where the world's first coffee beans were grown.

Now, five years later, Sal was at home in his bare but cozy little house that was nothing like the elaborate architecture he was used to in his Yemen village. However, it was comfortable, and it was now his permanent home. Or at least it would be, once he came back from serving in the army. He had enlisted the day before. If Sal got back safely, he would be a naturalized citizen of the United States. The war had been raging for months, and he wanted to fight for his new country. It was the right thing to do. It was how Sal's adoptive home would become his only home.

Sal's story is similar to the stories of many other Yemeni Americans who immigrated to the United States as long ago as 1890. Most Yemeni Americans came to the United States seeking economic opportunities—pursuing better lives for their families rather than fleeing wars and political and religious persecution like so many others from the region. Since there were not many Yemeni people in America at that time, they usually settled in communities of other Arabic speakers from Lebanon or Syria. Still, they often felt like outsiders.

Yemen is one of the oldest centers of civilization in the Arabian region. Its natural resources, excellent farmlands, and strategic location made it a target for invaders and fortune seekers from Persia and Rome in the ancient world and the Turkish and British Empires in more modern times. Two of Yemen's borders are on the Arabian and Red Seas; the other two are the countries of Saudi Arabia and Oman. It is an area brimming with history and a favorite among religious scholars. Admiration for Yemen is documented in ancient references. The Greek geographer Ptolemy referred to Yemen as "Arabia Felix," meaning "fortunate" and "happy."

The Queen of Sheba

One of the most famous historical figures is the Yemeni Queen of Sheba. The story of the Queen of Sheba, ancient ruler of lands located in what is now Yemen or Ethiopia, appears in religious texts sacred to Jews, Christians, and Muslims. She is referred to as Bilqis in the Qur'an and was known for her great wisdom, wealth, and beauty. Her story has inspired many legends. Historians believe the queen lived about 1,000 years before Jesus Christ was born. Under the Queen of Sheba's rule, Yemen was at its most prosperous and was at the cutting edge of agricultural technology. Yemeni people had developed an advanced irrigation system that enabled the watering of large expanses of fertile land all at once. Yemen was known for raising wonderful herbs and spices such as myrrh and frankincense. The Yemenis were also great traders and controlled the lucrative spice and aromatics trade of the region, which led to even more riches.

The best-known story of the queen is about how she matched wits with King Solomon during her visit to Jerusalem. As was the custom among heads of state in those days, she gave him impressive gifts; wondrous presents arrived from Yemen even before the queen's visit. Satisfied at the way he conducted affairs of state, she returned to her country and shared what she had learned. Historians believe that the Queen of Sheba may have been from either the Yemeni kingdom of Saba or the Ethiopian kingdom of Axum. They base their research on the fact that she took bales of incense with her as gifts, a type of frankincense that was only grown in those two regions.

Sculpt Coasters with Yemeni Frieze Designs

Some Yemeni Americans came from the World Heritage City of Sana'a, capital of Yemen and one of the oldest cities in the world. It is thought to have been founded by Noah, of biblical fame. Many of the houses are almost 1,500 years old. They are several stories high and have flat roofs. The elaborate friezes, fancy carved frames, and stained-glass windows make the ancient skyscraper houses look like giant chocolate and vanilla wedding cakes. A frieze is a decorated strip of molding usually sculpted onto a building.

What You Need

Adult supervision required

Newspapers

Oven

Covered work area

10-ounce package of terra-cotta oven-bake clay, such as Sculpey

Rolling pin

Ruler

3-by-5-inch index card

Plastic clay knife

Damp paper towels for wiping hands

10-ounce package of white oven-bake clay, such as Sculpey

Baking tray or cookie sheet

What You Do

1. Preheat the oven to 275°F.

2. For each coaster, take about a quarter of the terracotta clay and knead it until it is soft and smooth. Form it into a ball.

3. Use the rolling pin to flatten out each ball into a rectangular shape about ⅛-inch thick—use the index card as a guide.

4. Put the index card on top of your slab and trim around the edges with the clay knife so that the slab is the same size as

the card. Smooth, adding more bits of clay if necessary, to make sure the surface is even. Make all four coasters; then set them aside and clean the terracotta off your hands.

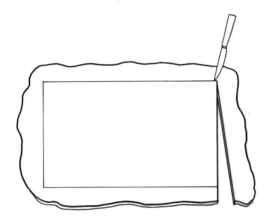

5. Knead a third of the white clay into a very long and very thin snaky rope. Use the clay knife to cut it into ¼-inch sections.

6. Make a triangle with white clay that will fit into each corner of the terra-cotta rectangle. Do not tamp the white clay down—let it rest on top.

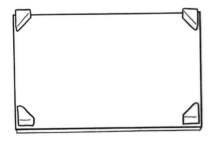

7. Use the rest of the white clay to make curved, lattice, or crisscross designs around all four sides. Make sure all four sides match. Leave the middle undecorated so that a glass will fit inside your design. You can make all four coasters the same or different. When you are satisfied with all of your designs, press down lightly on the white clay so that the design will stick but the colors do not blend together.

8. Place the coasters on the cookie sheet and put it in the oven for 10 minutes. Remove the cookie sheet from the oven and cool for half an hour. The coasters will be fragile, so handle them with care.

Some Yemeni immigrants got their American citizenship by fighting for the United States in 20th-century wars, beginning with World War I. To become a citizen at that time, immigrants had to be able to read, at least in their own language. However, even without this skill, one could still become a citizen by serving in the United States military. This enabled many immigrants who could not read or write to become Americans.

Some Yemeni newcomers settled in New York City, working as vendors or in coffee houses or shipyards. Others toiled in the steel mills of Buffalo, New York. Many moved west to the San Joaquin Valley of California, to work in the agriculture industry, where they could use the farming skills they had gained from Yemen's rich farming tradition. Other farmers became homesteaders. They lived on and cultivated plots of land that were usually far from any towns or villages. Life was often lonely for these men, who usually did not come with their families.

Cook Melon Baal Canaf (Melons with Wings)

Melon *baal canaf* (melon with wings) is a popular Yemeni dish that is said to disappear as soon as it is placed on the table, as though it had wings and flew away!

What You Need

Adult supervision required

Oven

Cutting board

Knife

3 small cantaloupes

Large bowl

2-quart baking dish

Stove

⅓ cup vegetable oil

Large skillet

1 pound ground chicken or turkey

1 teaspoon salt

2 cups chopped green onions

⅓ cup chopped parsley

¼ cup fresh lemon juice

2 cups cooked rice

Makes six ½-melon servings

What You Do

1. Preheat the oven to 350°F.

2. Cut each cantaloupe in half. Remove and discard the seeds and scoop the pulp out into a bowl, being careful to not cut the melon skin. Chop the melon pulp on the cutting board. Place the six cantaloupe "bowls" in the baking dish.

3. Heat the oil in a skillet and add the chicken or turkey. Add the salt and sauté until the poultry is done, about 15 minutes.

4. Add the onions, parsley, and lemon juice, and cook until the onions are soft, about 5 minutes. Remove from the heat and let cool.

5. Add the rice to the cooled poultry mixture in the pan and mix well. Stuff the mixture into the cantaloupe bowls. Spread a cup of the chopped melon pulp over the mixture. Bake for 20 minutes. Serve hot.

One of the most notable stories about how Yemeni people started life in the United States involves their employment at the Ford factory in Dearborn, Michigan. Henry Ford had visited Yemen in the early 1900s and was impressed with the way Yemeni people, like other Arab people he had encountered and hired, worked so hard. He encouraged them to come to Michigan, where they were paid five dollars an hour for their work on the auto assembly line. That was a lot of money in those days, and the automobile workers had steady work making cars. For the first time since the car was invented, everyday Americans, not just the wealthy, could afford to buy vehicles. As soon as the cars rolled off the assembly line, they were sold. Today, Yemeni Americans make up almost 10 percent of Dearborn's Arabic population. Because of the decline of the auto industry, many have chosen other professions. In Dearborn's South End neighborhood, Yemeni Americans own half of the stores. Many work for Great Lakes shipping companies.

Yemeni Americans are very active in work-related unions such as the United Farm Workers or the Service Employees International Union in California, providing leadership in both the agricultural industry and janitorial services. They join with others to improve working conditions. In recent times, unions have enlisted the help of Yemeni Americans to translate and to inform workers of their rights.

Nagi Daifallah (circa 1949–1973)

Nagi Daifallah, an artist and farm worker activist, played an important role in the farmworkers' struggle for equality. He was a great admirer of the United States Constitution and believed that all Americans should have the rights guaranteed by the Constitution. Daifallah's art showed the horrible working conditions of his fellow farmworkers. Because he spoke Spanish, English, and Arabic fluently, he translated for workers and authorities and was elected a strike captain during the United Farm Workers' grape strike. On August 15, 1973, he joined in a peaceful protest. However, law enforcement officers began to attack protesters, and Daifallah lost his life.

Some Yemini Americans are highly educated and skilled professionals working in hospitals, universities, and government agencies. They serve their communities through organizations such as the American Association of Yemeni Scientists and Professionals, which encourages higher education in Yemeni American communities. Yemeni Americans bring the beauty of the unique designs and architecture famous in their country of origin, as well as a rich array of cultures and traditions.

Although most are Muslim, there are also Christian and Jewish Yemeni Americans. Almost 20,000 Yemeni Americans live in the United States, in cities such as Dearborn, Michigan; Brooklyn and Buffalo, New York; Washington, DC; and Oakland, California. Dearborn kids have fun at the Yemen American Benevolence Association, where they learn to speak Arabic and get involved in helping their neighborhoods.

Dr. Nasser Zawia (contemporary)

An expert in the field of toxicology, Dr. Nasser Zawia is a professor in the Department of Pharmacology and the Division of Environmental Health at Meharry Medical College in Nashville, Tennessee. His research reflects his concerns about the effects of environmental toxins on brain development. He has been an advisor for both Tennessee and the National Institute for Environmental Health Sciences.

Play Oh Hillcock, Oh Hillcock

The Yemeni people have a rich poetry heritage. A traditional poetry game for girls, this game can be a challenge to write rap/poetry quickly and spontaneously. You make up the rhymes as you go along. None of the poems can be written ahead of time.

What You Need

An even number of friends divided into two teams

Pencils

Scraps of paper

Bag or bucket

Open area

Instrumental music

What You Do

1. Have everyone write down a topic on a piece of paper, fold it so no one can see it, and drop it into the bag or bucket. Themes can be anything: the moon, school, pets, friends, and so on.

2. Choose two teams and face each other in two lines.

3. Select a poet for each team. You can have the same poet or take turns going down the line.

4. Agree on which team will start—that team draws the "theme" from the bag. Both teams use the same topic.

5. Turn on the music. Stamp your feet and clap your hands to the beat.

6. The first poet recites her "rap" to the music, making it up as she goes along.

7. The poet for the other team goes next, keeping the beat going with hands and feet.

8. The first team who can't come up with a rhyme on its turn loses.

Hagage Abdul-Gowee Masaed (contemporary)

Born and raised in Ohio, Hagage Abdul-Gowee Masaed is a hip-hop artist known as AJ. He blends modern rap with traditional Arabic instruments like the *mizmar*, which is similar to a clarinet, and the oud, which resembles a fat banjo. AJ uses music to promote a message of peace in his family's home country of Yemen, where he is called the Godfather of Rap.

Say It in Yemeni

Many Americans learning Arabic learn the Yemen dialect, as it is easily understood throughout the Arab world. Yemeni Arabic retains many of the features of the traditional and universal written Arabic. So even the Yemeni Arabic that is spoken every day is very close to the Arabic used on formal occasions.

The old saying "A friend is found at a time of hardship" originated in Yemen. It may be the root of a similar saying in the United States, "A friend in need is a friend indeed."

> Assadeeq inda addeeq assadeeq: A friend is found at
> a time of hardship.
> a friend: As-SA-deek
> is found at: INda
> a time of hardship: a-DEEK

Notable Yemeni Americans

Raja Althaibani (1985–)   A photojournalist, community organizer, and freelance journalist for CNN, NPR, BBC, and MSNBC. She also worked as an AmeriCorps volunteer, helping new Arab immigrants.

Ali Baleed Almaklani (contemporary)   The cofounder and director of the Yemeni American Benevolent Association (YABA) in Dearborn, Michigan. YABA provides social and educational services and builds intercultural ties with Yemeni Americans and their neighbors.

Dr. Rashid A. Abdu (contemporary)   A surgeon, he founded the Joanie Abdu Comprehensive Breast Care Center in Ohio to help women stricken with breast cancer. He is also the author of *Journey of a Yemen Boy*.

First Sergeant Jamal S. Baadani (circa 1973–)   US Marine Corps (Ret.), and president of the Association of Patriotic Arab Americans in Military.

Brian Mihtar (1980–)   Michigan-based boxer nicknamed the Lion and known for his high percentage of knockout victories.

8

Arab Americans from the African Continent:

Moroccan, Tunisian, Algerian, and Libyan Americans

"What in the world is that?" The indigenous people were startled by the strange humped beast that came barreling through the Arizona desert. Like most people in the Americas, they had never seen such a weird animal. Atop the curious creature rode a man with a skin tone similar to theirs, but he was wearing brightly colored clothing—unlike the dull colors of the US military uniforms. First the Pueblo peoples had to endure the Europeans and later the

Americans invading their territory, and now this strange, snorting, spitting animal with a hump?

In 1856, the American military imported 75 camels from Algeria, Tunisia, Turkey, and Egypt to carry supplies and soldiers through the Southwestern desert along the path of today's famous Route 66 highway. And along with the camels came their handlers, camel drivers from those countries. The American soldiers were not used to the camels, which were not always as cooperative as horses. The Arab camel drivers tried to teach the Americans how to manage the huge animals, but the soldiers were not comfortable riding or handling them. To worsen matters, the army didn't pay the Arab men for their hard work, and most of them returned to the Middle East, leaving the camels with inexperienced owners who had little respect for their historical significance. One "camel whisperer" remained and became a legend in the Southwest. Hadji Ali came to be known as "Hi Jolly" and died in Quartzville, Arizona, in 1903. The state of Arizona built a memorial to him and the story of the camel escapade. Legend has it that a few of the camels escaped and some of their descendants are still roaming the Southwest!

The Camel

Green spit! Have you heard that camels spit? They don't really spit like people do; rather, they burp up some of their undigested food (like green slimy grass) and spray it out of their mouths at whomever makes them mad. They are ruminants like cows, which means they digest their food in one of their stomachs, creating "cud," and then they vomit it up and chew it again. Arab camels are dromedaries and have one hump.

Camels have thrived in some of the world's harshest environments. They can travel longer distances than most animals and can withstand long periods without water. When they do drink, they can store water for a long time. They eat almost anything and have few predators. Dromedary camels are most closely associated with Arabian lands, where they are domesticated. They have provided meat, milk, wool, and transportation for different Middle Eastern peoples for thousands of years. In the past, great caravans of 20,000 camels traveled across the desert carrying silk and spices. That's why camels have sometimes been called the ships of the desert. Camel trains still transport salt across the great Sahara, led by Berber guides who chart the journey with great precision. They know every watering hole and how to avoid the searing heat of the desert. In most places, the caravans have been replaced by trucks, but camels are still very important to cultures such as the Tuareg.

Camels have their place in American life, too. They are part of Christmas Nativity scenes, having carried the three wise men to the place where Jesus was born. Latino kids celebrate Three Kings Day and leave hay for the camels like kids leave cookies for Santa. Dr. Bob, a founder of Alcoholics Anonymous, introduced the animal as a symbol of staying sober and not drinking in this poem:

The camel each day goes twice to his knees.
He picks up his load with the greatest of ease.
He walks through the day with his head held high.
And stays for that day, completely dry.

Dr. Bob meant that people recovering from the disease of alcoholism should pray twice a day ("goes twice to his knees"), manage their burdens, be proud of being sober, and stay dry (don't drink alcohol). He was one American who had great affection for the camel.

Stitch a Camel Friend

You can keep a camel in your room! Sew this dromedary stuffed animal to keep you company.

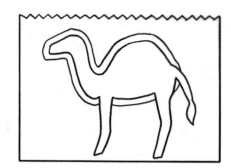

What You Need

Large brown paper bag to make a pattern

Pencil

Scissors

½ yard of brown felt

Straight pins

Fabric marker

2 white buttons for eyes, or googly eyes

Brown thread and needle

Stuffing, old cut-up rags, or old pantyhose

What You Do

1. Open up the paper bag and draw a camel outline, making it as large as you can. Cut it out.

2. Position your pattern on the felt so that you have enough room for two camels. Pin the pattern to the fabric and trace the first one. Move the pattern over and make a second outline, but do not trace the tail on the second camel. Cut out both camels.

3. Put one piece on top of the other, lining them up, so you can place the eyes evenly. Sew an eye onto each piece, and draw an ear on each piece, above and behind the eyes.

4. Then pin the pieces together with the eyes touching so you can't see them. Sew along the edges except for the legs and belly. Turn the camel right-side-out so the eyes show.

5. Stuff the camel with your stuffing material. Stitch up, but don't sew the legs together. Do not stuff the four legs or tail.

The first people to come to the United States from North African Arab countries were not the legendary camel drivers of the 1800s, but mariners from the region. Strange inscriptions in New England caves show that these early sailors may have visited Native Americans as early as 580 BCE. A tablet found on Long Island, New York, was assumed to be Indigenous American, but in 1973, a study revealed that the inscription is probably Libyan. There are accounts of Arab seamen in the 10th century sailing westward into what they named the Ocean of Darkness and Fog. Years later, they returned with wonderful treasures from what they called the strange and curious land of *Ard Majhoola*, Arabic for "unknown territory." Some think that Christopher Columbus may have been influenced to take his famous voyage after reading *The Sea of Darkness* by ash-Sharif al-Idrisi. It was a book about eight Arabs who sailed from Lisbon to explore what lay beyond the Atlantic Ocean. The book was found in Columbus's possessions after his death. Columbus is thought to have used the early Arab maps to chart his trip, and records indicate that there were Arab crew members on his vessels.

A Moroccan named Zammouri led a Spanish expedition into what is now the state of Florida in 1528. Eleven years later, Estevanico, an enslaved Moroccan who was probably a Berber, accompanied the Spaniard Marcos de Niza on his exploration of the Southwest and encountered Zuni people. Some stories say he was killed for helping bring the Europeans and their warlike ways to the area. Other legends say the Zuni people helped him fake his death so he could be free of his owners.

Most historians agree that the first Arab to settle permanently in the United States was from Algeria. In the 1700s, Wahab, along with his load of Arabian horses, was shipwrecked on Okracoke Island off the coast of North Carolina. He was supplying horses to the Continental Congress for use by the American Revolutionary forces. Wahab founded a settlement named Wahab Village; an inn is still run at the site by the Wahab family.

Some of the people captured and brought to America as slaves were from the Arabic countries located in Africa. About 7 percent of enslaved Africans were Muslim. There are stories of men and women who spoke Arabic and refused to eat pork (both Muslim and Jewish dietary laws ban pork). Most were forced to convert to Christianity, but in several Southern African American churches, Muslim customs such as building the church to face east and using prayer rugs were integrated with Christian rituals. Middle Eastern names like Aisha and Jamal are still popular in African American communities, probably handed down by Arab ancestors subjected to slavery. In 1790, South Carolina ruled that Moroccan Moors were to be tried in white courts instead of by the slave code. Although the decision did not free them, it recognized that they were Arab and subjects of the king of Morocco.

Over generations, these Arabic-speaking people lost most of their original culture and languages like most other descendants of enslaved peoples of the United States. Slave owners did not permit enslaved people to speak their own languages or practice their customs or religions—this was one way to weaken people and shatter their hopes of freedom. Imagine being kidnapped from your family, brought to a strange land on a crowded, dirty ship, beaten, chained, sold like livestock, and then punished for speaking your own language and praying. It destroyed the Arab culture among these victims of the slave trade. Today it is estimated that over 50,000 Americans have their origins in Morocco, Tunisia, Libya, and Algeria, but no one knows for sure.

Berbers

To members of the Catholic faith, Saint Augustine is a highly regarded saint. He lived in the fifth century and became a Catholic priest, writer, and philosopher, and he is considered one of the great thinkers of history. Saint Augustine was also a Berber. The Berbers are the indigenous people of North Africa, as Native Americans are the indigenous people of the United States. Like

Native Americans, they come from many different groups and have different languages and cultures. There are around 300 local dialects among the Berbers. It is estimated that there are 50 million Berbers worldwide. The preferred name for the Berber people, especially in Morocco, is Amazigh and their language is called Tamazight. People of Berber or Berber Arabic descent live in many places in the United States. In Philadelphia, Pennsylvania, the Berber American Community organization teaches the Berber language and culture to Berber American kids.

Berber communities are spread throughout Tunisia, Libya, Algeria, and Morocco, and there are some in Egypt, too. Many live in cities, but more often they live in the mountains and in small towns. They are mainly Muslims, but they still have traditional practices that predate Islam. Until recently, Berbers were looked down upon in the same way that other indigenous peoples in the world are treated. Today, Berbers are standing up for their rights, such as teaching the Berber languages, which at one time were forbidden, in schools. The Berbers have a strong history and founded several dynasties. In fact, the Moors from North Africa who ruled Spain for centuries were also Berber.

One group of Berbers is the Tuareg, desert dwellers from areas that include parts of West Africa. There are also Tuareg people in the United States. In the United States, Tuareg Americans usually dress like most other Americans, but in North Africa the dress customs differs from those of other Muslims. Instead of women wearing veils, it is customary for Tuareg men to cover their faces. Although Berbers probably make up most of the population in the region, their cultures and languages are in the minority. Still they have influenced the lifestyle of North Africa in many ways, such as through musical traditions. Tunisian, Moroccan, Algerian, and Libyan Americans honor their heritage by featuring traditional songs in weddings and festivals. Many are from the Berber tradition. Berber instruments such as the *doumek* and *zill* are played in a type of music known as *gnawa*. *Gnawa* literally means "song" in Arabic and is the name given to percussion music played by North African instrumentalists.

Gnawa is loud, metallic, rhythmic, clangy music. *Karakebs* (also *qaraqebs* or *gargabas*) are large double castanets that set the rhythm. They look like dumbbells that have been cut lengthwise and hollowed out, then held together by leather string. Karakebs players hold a set in each hand. It takes years of practice to get the best tone.

Make Karakebs

Many American jazz musicians, such as Randy Weston, John Coltrane, and Dizzy Gillespie, studied the unique music scales from North African Arab countries. Make your own version of karakebs and make your own gnawa.

What You Need

Covered work area

Index card cut into 2 strips, 6 inches by 1 inch

Sturdy cardboard, 10 inches by 2 inches

Foil paper

Strong glue (such as Gorilla Glue)

4 quarters

Stapler

Paint

Paintbrushes

Water to clean the brushes

What You Do

1. Fold the two strips cut from the index card in half the long way so that each is 3 inches high. This will be called a V-strip.

2. Wrap the V-strip with foil paper and glue the foil paper in place.

3. Glue two quarters facing each other on the inside of both V-strips, right near the opening. Make sure the quarters meet up when the open ends of the V-strips are held together. This will ensure the best sound. Let the glue dry completely.

4. Staple one V-strip to each end of the cardboard. Paint designs on the cardboard and the V-strips (but not on the coins) and let dry.

5. To play the karakebs, hold the cardboard "handle" in one hand and slap the V-strip against your other palm, alternating the top V-strip and the bottom one to make a rhythm.

Malika Zarra (contemporary)

A clang of karakeb, a strum of oud, a tinkling of piano, and a scat of jazz singing, but in Berber! Moroccan American jazz singer and composer Malika Zarra arrived in New York City from France with her Arabic instruments and her love of jazz, true American music. A key element of jazz is improvisation, or the art of making up music on the spot. Improvisation is a big part of Moroccan music, too, so jazz really appealed to Malika. Not only did she travel from Morocco, to France, to the United States, but in her workshops, she teaches kids how music travels around the world, too. In her family, music was part of everyday activities, but she did not study music until she learned to play the clarinet at age 19. Sometimes she writes songs; other times she teaches musicians how to play the tricky Moroccan rhythms. On stage, Malika serenades her fans in Berber, Moroccan Arabic, French, and English.

Languages in North African Arab Countries

The languages of North African countries reflect many different cultures. Arabic is used as the main written and official language. Various combined Arab and Berber dialects are used in everyday conversation, and many words are borrowed from European languages. French is taught and used in many schools. Because a great number of them are fluent in French, North African Arabs mainly emigrated to France and not the Americas.

Say It in Moroccan

Here are some everyday Moroccan words borrowed from different places.

Cat	Berber: (Amouch)	Moroccan: mujj (Mouch)
Telephone	French: téléphone (tay-lay-FUN)	Moroccan: tilifūn (the-leh-FUHN)
Kitchen	Spanish: cocina (co-CHEE-na)	Moroccan: cuzina (ku-ZEE-nah)
Beach	Portuguese: praia	Moroccan: blaya (blah-yah)
Cookies	German: kekse (kayk-suh)	Moroccan: kekse (keks-kee)

Morocco

Morocco is at the northern tip of Africa, bordering the North Atlantic Ocean and the Mediterranean Sea, between Algeria and the Western Sahara. There are rich agricultural plains along the coastline and mountains in the interior part of the country. There are only about eight miles between Morocco and Spain. From 711 to 1492, Arab Muslim Moors ruled Spain and introduced modern medicine, farming techniques, great architecture, and literature to what was then called Al-Andalus. They founded the University of Salamanca, the first college in Europe. For most of that time, the people enjoyed religious tolerance and respect. However, in 1492, Spanish Catholic rulers Queen Isabel and King Ferdinand reconquered Islamic Spain and immediately forced Muslims and Jews to convert to Christianity. This was called the Inquisition. However, most Jews were expelled by the new powers that very year—many fled to Morocco. The Ottoman Empire (Turkey) sent ships to rescue Jews and Muslims. After suffering years of religious persecution, the Muslims were finally expelled in 1609. Today there is still a strong Arabic Islamic influence on Spanish culture.

The New United States Is Recognized as a Country

A very old country was the first to extend friendship to a very young country. On December 20, 1777, Morocco formally recognized the American colonies as a sovereign nation, the United States of America. It was the first country to do so. In 1787, the US Congress passed the Treaty of Peace and Friendship between the two nations, and it is the longest unbroken treaty relationship in US history. The American Legation in Tangier, Morocco, was granted to the United States in 1821, making it the oldest American diplomatic property in a foreign country. Today it is a museum and a national historic landmark.

People of the Jewish faith were the first Moroccans to move to the United States in large numbers. Some had left Morocco searching for a way out of poverty and traveled to South America to work in the newly developing rubber business. When that industry fell apart in 1910, many came north to the United States. More Moroccans arrived after World War II.

Other Moroccans did not emigrate in significant numbers until the 1990s. Most of these were highly skilled professionals or students. Because Europe is so close to Morocco, unskilled workers have gone there to find work, much like Latino people from Mexico and Central America travel to the United States in search of employment. In the United States, Moroccans live in many different states. In New York City and Washington, DC, special organizations preserve Moroccan culture and community. Today there are almost 40,000 Moroccan Americans. In the popular Disney movie *Holes*, the character of Zero is played by Khleo, a rapper and actor of Moroccan Jewish ancestry. Have you ever worn a Guess watch or Guess Jeans? Paul Marciano, a fashion designer and the owner of Guess, Inc., also has ties to the Moroccan Jewish community.

Create a Pair of Belgha Slippers

Moroccan artisans are known for their soft slippers, many of which have beautiful and colorful decorations.

What You Need

2 pieces of paper large enough to make a pattern
of each foot, with room left over

Pencil

Scissors

2 heavy-duty felt rectangles, 9 inches by 12 inches
by ¼ inch (for soles)

Straight pins

2 regular felt squares, 9 inches by 12 inches (for tops)

Ruler

Felt glue, such as Beacon

Fabric paint, any color

What You Do

1. For the soles of the slippers, stand on the paper and have someone trace the outline of each of your feet, leaving a 1-inch margin all the way around. Cut out both feet. Write "L Sole" on the left pattern and "R Sole" on the right pattern.

2. For the tops of your slippers, place each sole pattern on a larger sheet of paper and draw an outline for just the top half of each foot, making it 3 inches larger around the curved sections. Cut out. Write "L Top" and "R Top" on these patterns. Set aside.

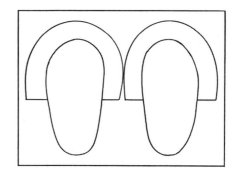

3. Lay the sole patterns on the thicker felt squares and use straight pins to secure. Lay the slipper top patterns on the lighter-weight felt. You will need two tops and two soles. Cut out and write very lightly what each one is so you don't lose track: "L S," "R S," "L T," "R T."

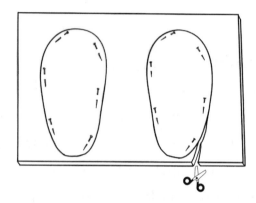

4. On each top, draw lines that are 1 inch apart and ½ inch long. Cut on these lines—these flaps help you fit the top onto the bottom of your slipper and give when you walk so the slipper won't break.

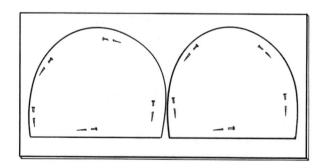

5. Center the tops onto the soles and turn over. Starting at the toe, wrap the flaps around the bottom of the sole and glue down each flap with felt glue.

6. When the glue has set, move the sole to the right and glue down the flaps on the right-hand side. When the right side has set, move the sole to the left and repeat with that side.

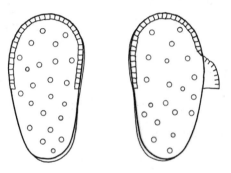

7. Make polka dots with fabric paint on the bottoms of the soles so they won't slip. Let dry. You can decorate the slippers with sequins, beads, or fabric paint.

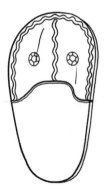

Notable Moroccan Americans

Tarik Banzi (contemporary)   Musician and director of
Al-Andalus Ensemble, whose music blends Flamenco
and Ladino (Jewish-Spanish) melodies with Arabic
rhythms.

Sanaa Hamri (1975–)   A music video and film direc-
tor, she has worked with Jay-Z, A*Teens, Christina
Aguilera, and Mariah Carey. One of her films, *Just
Wright*, starred Queen Latifah.

Dr. Laila Lalami (1968–)   First Moroccan author to
publish an English book of fiction in the United
States and a professor at the University of California–
Riverside.

Adil Oualim (1965–)   Founder and director of New
York's Moroccan American House, an organization
that helps Moroccan immigrants and teaches
children Arabic and Moroccan culture.

Khalid Khannouchi (1971–)   A marathon runner, he
broke the marathon world record twice, and is one
of only four men who ever broke their own records.

Algeria

Algeria borders the Mediterranean Sea between Tunisia and
Morocco, and the Sahara Desert covers 80 percent of the country.
Algeria is Arabic for "the islands," probably referring to the rocky
islands strung along the coastline. The official language is Arabic,
but Berber and French are also spoken. Algeria was colonized by
France and gained its sovereignty (independence) in 1962. Most
of the people are a mixture of Arab and Berber. Berber people
include different groups, such as the Kabyles, the Chaouia, and the
Tuareg, all of whom have resisted colonization since ancient times.

From 1821 to 1830, fewer than 20 Algerians are recorded to
have immigrated to the United States. However, as was the case
with other peoples from the Middle East, immigrants were often
labeled Turks, so the records are not accurate. It wasn't until 1975
that a separate category for Algerians was listed on immigration
documents. Today it is estimated that there are around 4,000
Algerian Americans. Most live in the urban centers of New York
City, Miami, Washington, and Los Angeles, but students and pro-
fessors also live in university communities such as Dallas
and Boston.

Notable Algerian Americans

Yasmine Amanda Bleeth (1968–)Actress, most famous for her role as Caroline Holden in the television series *Baywatch*.

Frédéric Fekkai (1958–)   Hairstylist and entrepreneur who has done the hair of prominent women including Secretary of State Hilary Clinton and actress Jessica Lange, among others. His hair care products are sold in stores across America.

Hocine Khalfi (1928–2011)   Boxer called the Golden Glove. Before he moved to the United States, he was the featherweight champ of Algeria.

Larry Pierce Williams (1930–1979)   A descendant of Wahab, the first Algerian in the United States. Williams was the founder and first president of the Ocracoke Preservation Society, which preserves the culture of Ocracoke Island.

Dr. Elias A. Zerhouni (1951–)   Director of the National Institutes of Health from 2002 to 2008.

Zaida Ben-Yusuf (1869–1933)

"Hold that pose!" Zaida Ben-Yusuf was a famous 19th-century American photographer. She became one of the most creative and sought-after fashion and portrait photographers of her time and is credited with turning photography into an art form. Working as a professional photographer in those days was unusual, especially for women, and she faced many challenges. But Zaida Ben-Yusuf's pictures graced the covers of magazines across the nation, and she even wrote about her craft for national newspapers. Famous people such as Franklin Roosevelt sat for her, too. Her work was exhibited all over the world, and in 2008, 75 years after her death, Zaida Ben-Yusuf's works were featured in a special show at the Smithsonian's National Portrait Gallery, "Zaida Ben-Yusuf: New York Portrait Photographer."

Snap a Photograph in Zaida Ben-Yusuf's Style

Zaida Ben-Yusuf's photos look very mysterious—her models are rarely smiling. The backgrounds are dark and often make the people look as if they are floating. Sometimes the models hold a prop such as a branch, and the photos often have just a hint of a nature scene in the background.

What You Need

Paper

Pencil

Scenery for background: a curtain, artwork, or blank wall

Lights

Model(s)

Unusual clothing for the model to wear: big hats, scarves, boas, elaborate dresses

Camera with the ability to take black-and-white pictures or a disposable black-and-white camera

What You Do

1. Sketch your ideas for a portrait—this is not a candid shot, but a very planned photograph.

2. Build your set or background. Experiment with the lights to get different effects. The less light, the more mysterious; more light makes it look like daylight, etc. Have your model put on some interesting clothing items— you can use some of the projects in this book to create things for him or her to wear.

3. Pose your model and snap away, but don't let him or her smile!

Tunisia

Anakin Skywalker's home is in Tunisia! The building used to portray young Anakin's home in the *Star Wars* movies is a *ksar*, an ancient grain storage castle in southern Tunisia. Director George Lucas thought the spot was just perfect for the *Episode I: The Phantom Menace* and *Episode IV: A New Hope* films in his famous *Star Wars* movie series. But Tunisia is not in a galaxy far, far away, and there are lessons to be learned from the architecture of Tunisia's peoples. Centuries ago, this once-huge storage complex housed grains and oils, keeping them fresh for up to six years!

Today these ancient buildings are the site of a bustling bazaar, where one can appreciate the art of the country.

Tunisia is known for its crafts heritage. Women weave carpets called *mergoums* with a bold diamond pattern, and *klims*, which are woven with alternate strips of natural-colored wools. Contemporary Tunisian artists have brought back the ancient art of glass blowing and decorating. Glass was invented in Arabia centuries ago. Many of the artisans decorate the exquisite glassware with colorful designs of geometric shapes and plants.

Design a Dried-Flower Serving Plate

Love is in the air! Jasmine is a romantic flower as well as the national flower of Tunisia. If a man wears it over his left ear, it lets everyone know he is single. If he offers a jasmine flower to a special friend, it is seen as proof of love. The fragrant and delicate bloom opens only at night. It can be picked in the morning, when the flower is tightly closed, and kept in a cool place until evening, when the beautiful petals open up and make the whole house smell wonderful. In Tunisia, young boys make small bouquets and sell them to drivers stopped at intersections.

What You Need

Adult supervision required

Covered work area

2 clear glass plates of the same size, the flatter the better

2 paper towels

2 glazed ceramic tiles, 3 inches by 3 inches

2 coffee filters (any kind)

Two jasmine flowers with part of the stem and, if possible, a few leaves still attached (Pansies or petunias can also be used)

Microwave

Oven mitts

Scissors

Clear glue that can be used for glass

Acrylic paint in colors of your choice

Paintbrushes

Transparent all-weather waterproof tape or clear duct tape

What You Do

1. Remove any stickers from the plates, wash them, dry them, and set them aside.

2. Put one paper towel over one of the tiles, shiny side up. Place a coffee filter on top of the towel. Make a pattern with the flowers and leaves without overlapping any of them.

Cover with the second coffee filter, followed by the second paper towel.

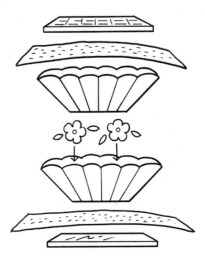

3. Place the second tile on top with the shiny side facing down, so you have a flower "sandwich." Carefully place the sandwich in the microwave and cook at 50 percent or half power for 20 seconds. Remove with the oven mitts.

4. Carefully lift the top tile, paper towel, and filter to check the flowers. If they look dry, you can continue to the next step. If they are not dry enough, cover the flowers as before and return everything to the microwave. Dry at half power or on the defrost setting for just 10 seconds at a time, checking after each interval. Be careful, as they can burn.

5. When the flowers are dry, remove the tile sandwich from the microwave and take off the top tile, paper towel, and filter. Carefully arrange a design in the center of one of the plates. Attach it with a few dabs of glue. Paint designs around the rim of the plate. When the paint is dry, add more dabs of glue around the plate edge.

6. Nest the second plate on top of the decorated plate so the flower design is in another "sandwich." Carefully hold both plates together until the glue holds. When the plates are bonded to each other, seal the plate edges together all the way around with tape. You can use your jasmine plate to serve cookies, bread, or other foods that aren't moist. Wash the plate carefully—do not submerge it in water.

Tunisia is the northernmost country in Africa and is bordered by Algeria on the west, Libya to the southeast, and the Mediterranean Sea on the north and east. The Sahara Desert is in its southern region, but the rest of Tunisia is extremely fertile. During the time of the Roman Empire, it was labeled the bread basket of Rome for its rich agricultural culture. In 2011, Tunisians protested their government, which they saw as oppressive and unfair. This led to revolutions in many Arab countries during a period that is now called the Arab Spring or reawakening.

May 27 is Tunisian American Day! Organized in a different American city every year, it is celebrated with a *hafla* (party) for Ibn Khaldun's birthday. He is the cultural symbol for the Tunisian American Community Center, which has chapters across the country. Ibn Khaldun lived hundreds of years ago (1332–1406) and is the father of sociology, the study of human civilizations. The celebration includes the Ibn Khaldun Award presentation, which honors individuals for their work in the Tunisian American community. The communities tend to be small because although many Tunisians come to the United States to study, most go home when their education is completed.

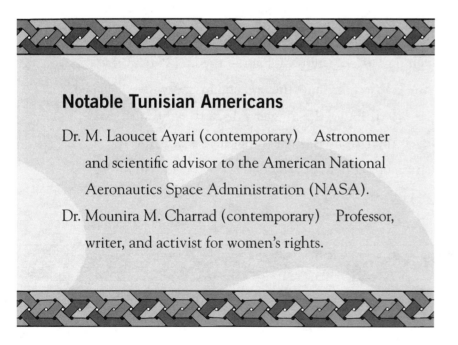

Notable Tunisian Americans

Dr. M. Laoucet Ayari (contemporary)   Astronomer and scientific advisor to the American National Aeronautics Space Administration (NASA).

Dr. Mounira M. Charrad (contemporary)   Professor, writer, and activist for women's rights.

King of Birds

Once the lion and the kinglet, a very tiny bird, were threatening each other and bragging of their strength and courage.

"I can kill you with just a wave of my paw," boasted the lion.

"And I'll break your head over my knee first," the bird answered.

After going back and forth with bigger and bigger boasts, they challenged each other to a great battle to prove their claims. The lion called on all the creatures on Earth that walked and did not fly, and the kinglet gathered every creature that traveled on wings. The fighting began.

"Attack the lion about the head!" the kinglet commanded. The mosquitoes and gnats answered his cry by the thousands and buzzed around the lion's ears and eyes so he couldn't see. He crashed into the foxes and hyenas, screaming, "Let's flee!"

"Charge the cattle!" the kinglet ordered next, and the oxflies and gadflies ambushed the camels and donkeys. Soon the animals were running in confusion, trying to escape the insects' bites.

The kinglet made matters worse as she carried burning embers on her tail and sprayed them on the animals, yelling, "Ittfou! Ittfou!" ("Put out the fire! Put out the fire!") In a short time, the lion and his army were defeated.

To this day, the kinglet calls, "Ittfou, ittfou!" And even though she is tiny and her nest is only the size and shape of a coffee cup, the Tunisians consider her the king of birds.

Libya

Libya is the fourth-largest country on the African continent. It borders Algeria and Tunisia in the west, Egypt and Sudan in the east, and Niger and Chad in the south. On the north, it has 1,100 miles of coastline on the Mediterranean Sea. The fertile coastline of the north is very different from the vast Sahara Desert in the south. Over its long history, Libya has been invaded and colonized by several different countries, including Turkey, Italy, and France. In the late 1700s and early 1800s, Tripoli, the capital of Libya, was controlled by the Barbary pirates, who demanded payment from foreign ships to sail and trade in the area. The United States negotiated several treaties with the pirates and even got into armed conflicts with them, known as the Barbary Wars. In the Marine Corps anthem, the "Marines' Hymn," the line "To the shores of Tripoli" refers to the First Barbary War.

Many Libyan Americans never intended to leave home. They were forced to flee because they spoke out against the government of Libyan president Muammar Gadhafi, who ruled the country for over 30 years. Rapper Khaled M's father was jailed for being an activist. He managed to escape the country, but throughout Khaled M's childhood the family moved from one place to another, trying to find somewhere safe to live. They finally joined other exiled Libyans in Lexington, Kentucky, where they built a community, worked, and raised their children. When the Libyan revolution broke out in 2011, some Libyan Americans returned to their home country to aid in the struggle. And Khaled M helped the cause with his song "Can't Take Our Freedom." One verse says, "When the regime just seems so unstoppable / When freedom feels like it's impossible / The people rise and overcome every obstacle."

Libyans, like other immigrants, have added their special flavors to American cuisine. Today, couscous is a favorite dish for many Americans and can be found in grocery stores across the country.

Cook Couscous

Couscous is a semolina-based staple food of Tunisia, Morocco, Libya, and Algeria. It is considered a healthier grain than most pastas and is served with vegetables, beef, lamb, chicken, fish, and sometimes camel meat stews. In different North African countries, archaeologists discovered couscous-making tools dating back to the ninth century. The first written reference to couscous appeared in a 13th-century Moroccan-Spanish cookbook.

The word *couscous* comes from the Berber word *sesku*, which means well-formed and well-rounded. Couscous has various names in the different parts of the North African region and has spread far beyond the African borders to the rest of the world. Couscous is used in main dishes and sometimes even sweetened to make desserts similar to rice pudding. In Libya, couscous is called *ta'am*, the Arabic word for "food," which shows just how important it is to the Libyans.

What You Need

Adult supervision required

½ cup cold water

¼ cup raisins

Small bowl

Stove

Saucepan with lid

2 tablespoons olive oil

1 tablespoon finely chopped onion

¼ cup diced red bell pepper

Two cups dry couscous

3 cups water

1 teaspoon salt

½ teaspoon ground black pepper

Fork

¼ cup chopped parsley

Makes ten ½-cup side servings or five 8-ounce main-dish servings

What You Do

1. Put the ½ cup of cold water and the raisins into a small bowl and set aside.

2. In the saucepan, heat the olive oil over medium-low heat. Add the onion and bell pepper and sauté for two minutes or until the onions are softened. Remove from the heat and add the couscous, water, and salt and pepper.

3. Drain the raisins and add them to the saucepan. Cover the saucepan and place it over medium-high heat until the water comes to a boil. Reduce the heat and simmer for 10 minutes.

4. Remove the pan from the heat and keep it covered for at least 20 minutes, until the couscous has absorbed all the water. Remove the lid, add the parsley, and fluff up with a fork before serving.

Notable Libyan Americans

Aly Ramadan Abuzaakouk (contemporary) President of the Citizenship Forum for Human Development and Democracy and the editor of *Democracy Watch*.

Reem Gibriel (contemporary) Sculptor whose work often sends a strong message about what war and bombing do to innocent children, like in the 2008 bombing of Gaza.

Fadel Lamen (contemporary) Journalist, writer, and Middle East/North Africa expert and cultural adviser based in Washington. He is the director of the American-Libyan Council.

9

Arab Americans from Arabian Gulf Countries:

Saudi, Kuwaiti, Bahraini, Qatari, Emirati, and Omani Americans

The land mine detonated, spewing lethal fragments into the air. It should have hurt Jabbar, the young Saudi who had stepped on the buried bomb just seconds before. Instead, the explosion embedded a hidden gemstone in his skin that gave him superhuman strength and turned him into Jabbar the Powerful!

Samda the Invulnerable is a tiny eight-year-old girl, but no one can even touch her, as none can break through her force field. College student Noora the Light from the United Arab Emirates sees the light of truth in others and helps them to see it in themselves. And no door is closed to Fattah the Opener from Indonesia, who can transport himself and others across vast distances.

All these superheroes and 95 more are guided by Dr. Ramzi Razem, whose mission is to unite THE 99 and save the world from evil forces. *THE 99* is a comic book series. The superheroes come from many different countries throughout Europe, Asia, Africa, the

Middle East, and from the United States. Batina the Hidden from Yemen, who can make herself and anything she touches invisible, has secret meetings with Wonder Woman. Soon THE 99 and the Justice League of America will team up to rid the world of villains.

The 99 series was developed by Dr. Naif Al-Mutawa, who has homes in both Kuwait and the United States, where he was educated. As founder of the Teshkeel Media Group, he creates exciting animated television programs and comic books. He grew up on American comic books such as *Batman* and *Superman* and wanted his own children to enjoy comic books, too. But he wanted his kids to have some good Arab role models. The super-heroes of *THE* 99 are all young and based on Middle Eastern history and Islamic models who embody kindness, generosity, and helpfulness, among other values shared by all religions. Some of the world's most famous comic book artists work on the project. Dr. Al-Mutawa, a clinical psychologist, has created positive rep-resentations of Islam, and how better to communicate them to young readers than in a comic book? Published in eight languages, *THE* 99 has inspired a theme park in Jahra, Kuwait, the first ever in the Middle East. Dr. Al-Mutawa has won several awards for his humanitarian work, including the United Nations UNESCO prize for literature in the service of tolerance. President Barack Obama praised Dr. Al-Mutawa's *THE* 99 "for its ability to capture the imaginations of young people through a message of tolerance."

The story of *THE* 99 focuses on 99 gemstones that contain knowledge and power from the 13th-century Library of Wisdom in Baghdad, Iraq. When an enemy army invaded the country and threw thousands of books into the river, the horrified scholars saved the day. They threw gemstones into the water that absorbed all of the books' contents, preserving the knowledge forever. The gemstones were hidden across the earth—the stones themselves choose worthy carriers in modern times. Although the stones and carriers find each other, each person must decide whether to use his or her powers for good or evil. It is said that Allah (Arabic for God) has 99 attributes, such as mercy, wisdom, and compassion. The powers of *THE* 99 are loosely based on those values.

Become a Comic Book Artist

Kaboom! Did you know that the comic book style was inspired by Egyptian hieroglyphics? Cartoons and comic books have been part of the American media for almost 300 years.

The first cartoon was probably penned by Benjamin Franklin in 1754 and featured a snake with a severed head and the printed words "Join or Die." Franklin was urging the separate colonies to form what was to become the United States. At one time, comic books had funny themes, which is how the name "comics" or "funnies" came about. But writers soon realized that this form of expression could be used for serious subjects and stories, too. Once outlawed by educators, today comic books are used to get kids interested in reading through a program called the Comic Book Project. Turn your brain into a superpower and create your own comic book.

What You Need

Scrap paper

Pencil or pen

Blank index cards

Colored markers, colored pencils, or crayons

Notebook

Double-sided tape

Fine-point marker or pen

Super imagination!

What You Do

1. Think about the positive values that are important to you. Some examples are sharing, courage, cooperation, humility, and honesty. Some values are learned in religious teachings or from people we admire; others come from our families and schools. Pick three and write them down.

2. Think of three negative situations that are hurtful or unpleasant, such as bullying, selfishness, poverty, pollution, or illness. Write them down.

3. Imagine three superheroes—one for each value—and how they would eliminate or heal the negative situations. Write a

story about it. You can make yourself one of the superheroes, too! Imagine yourself as Pedro the Trustworthy, Maha the Tolerant, or Rachel the Just.

4. Go back and read your story, imagining the action. Eliminate as many words as you can, because the pictures will tell the story. Draw one scene on an index card—these are the "frames" for your comic book. Number them on the back to help keep them in order. Try to make at least 12 frames for your three characters and three situations. Tape them into your notebook to make a comic book—make sure you leave room to write around each frame. If you use double-sided tape, you can move the frames around.

5. With the fine-line marker or pen, write the text for each frame. When characters speak, put their words in a bubble, using as few words as possible. Comic books use many onomatopoeias, which are words that actually describe and sound like what they mean like "buzz," "clap," "achoo," or "plop." This cuts down on the number of words needed. Use this technique in your book—it's your creation, so you can make up your own words, too! Remember, the pictures will show the story. Decorate an index card with the name of your comic and attach it to the front of the book. *Wham!*

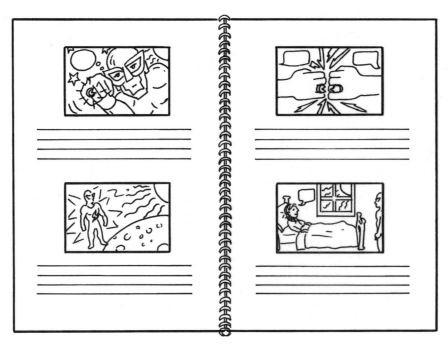

Like Dr. Al-Mutawa, other people from the Arabian Gulf area have homes in both the United States and their native countries. When people from the Gulf States finish their studies abroad, many go back to their countries, as their home governments give citizens great incentives to return.

Mostly surrounded by water, the Arabian Gulf area also features vast deserts where ancient Bedouin culture was strong. For centuries, the Bedouins traveled throughout the desert regions of the Middle East and Northern Africa with their herds of camels, sheep, and goats. *Bedouin* is the Arabic word for "desert dwellers." Although they did well living in harsh desert landscapes and moving from place to place, today most Bedouin live in permanent communities.

The countries that make up the Arabian Gulf States, located on the world's largest peninsula, are Saudi Arabia, Kuwait, Bahrain, Qatar, the United Arab Emirates, and Oman. Most of the people in these countries are Muslim. Kids join Girl Scout and Boy Scout troops like they do in the United States. Many Americans travel to the region to work. Just like people from the Arabian Gulf, they, too, travel back and forth. At least 25 percent of the people living in the area are foreign workers. Every able-bodied Muslim (including Muslim Arab Americans) is urged, if possible, to make the hajj—the pilgrimage to Mecca, Saudi Arabia, the holiest city in the Islamic religion and a place of great peace.

The Five Pillars of Islam

Structures are built on pillars that ensure that the building stays in place. Likewise, Islam has five pillars that Muslims follow to uphold their beliefs. The first and most important pillar is the Shahada. This literally means to bear witness and declare that there is "no God but one God and Muhammad is the prophet of God." Muslims admired the way that the prophet Muhammad lived. He was a wonderful man, father, husband, countryman, leader, and tradesman. He was fair and kind, helped the elderly and the poor, and ensured that women had full equal rights and the ability to own land and run their own businesses. He consulted women in military matters, and they also participated in battles.

The second pillar is prayer. Practicing Muslims offer five prayers each day, and they give special prayers on Fridays after a sermon. *Eid* celebrations and funeral prayers are also observed. The most important eids or festivals are Eid al-Fitr at the end of the holy month of fasting,

Ramadan, and Eid al-Adha after the hajj pilgrimage season. Muslims celebrate eids by visiting friends and family and eating special meals and desserts. Children wear new clothes and get gifts and money.

The third pillar is fasting. Muslims fast during the month of Ramadan, the ninth month on the Muslim lunar calendar based on the cycles of the moon. The Qur'an, or Muslim holy book, was first revealed to Muhammad by God during Ramadan. Even before Islam, Ramadan was a month when people fasted. Fasting exists in all faiths.

Muslims do not eat or drink during the daylight hours for the entire month of Ramadan, but children, the elderly, pregnant women, and the sick are not required to fast. The pinch of hunger that they experience reminds them to have compassion for those with no money or food or in less privileged circumstances. After sunset, Muslims eat and pray extra prayers. During Ramadan, Muslims read the Qur'an more frequently.

The fourth pillar of Islam is *zakat*, which is almsgiving. Every Muslim is required to give 2.5 percent of his or her income to charity each year. It is believed that if every Muslim gives the *zakat*, poverty will end.

The fifth pillar is hajj. This is the pilgrimage to the holy city of Mecca in Saudi Arabia that each person who is healthy and can afford to is urged to make at least once in his or her lifetime. Mecca is the birthplace of the prophet Muhammad, the birthplace of Islam, and the location of the Ka'aba, a cube-shaped building rebuilt by the prophet Abraham and his son. Muslims believe that the Ka'aba, which literally means "cube," was erected by Adam, the first man. All Muslims face it when they pray. At the corner of the Ka'aba is a black stone, believed to be a stone from heaven. Scientific studies have proven that it did not originate on Earth. It is believed that the black stone was pure white in color, but the sins of mankind made it black. Muslims walk around the Ka'aba seven times, saying. *"Labaika Allahumma Labaik,"* meaning, "We have answered your call, God." God ordered Abraham to call people to hajj, promising him that they would come by all forms of transportation. At the time, the area was just desert with no inhabitants, so it seemed impossible that thousands of people would be there. Muslims today heed that call, arriving by boat, car, and plane. They reflect on the important things in life and renew their faith. It is said that hajj wipes out all of a person's sins.

Saudi Arabia

Saudi Arabia is the largest of the Arabian Gulf countries. The Red Sea makes up its western boundary; Iraq, Jordan, and Kuwait are on the north; the Gulf of Arabia, Qatar, and the United Arab Emirates are its eastern edge; Oman is its southeastern neighbor, and Yemen shares its southwestern border. Saudi Arabia supplies much of the world's oil. The hajj draws over 2.5 million people annually and, after oil, earns the country the biggest part of its income. The area around the Ka'aba is constantly being expanded to accommodate the increasing number of Muslims who make the pilgrimage. The king of Saudi Arabia holds the title "custodian of the two holy shrines." It is considered an honor to maintain the sacred site, and once each year, members of the Saudi royal family wash the floors of the Ka'aba with rosewater. The hajj is the largest annual gathering of Muslims, who attend from every part of the world. American Muslims are welcomed visitors, too. The Ka'aba is at the center of the largest mosque in the world.

Saudi Arabia has many universities, but in the time before they were built, many young people went abroad to study. The Saudi government has shown its appreciation to American universities by giving them millions of dollars in education grants. Although many Saudis still study or work in other countries, most return home. People from many different places immigrate to the United States for a better life, but people in Saudi Arabia usually enjoy a comfortable lifestyle and do not often leave their country permanently and become citizens of other nations. There are about 5,000 Saudi Americans living in 42 states. California, Colorado, Florida, Pennsylvania, Texas, and Virginia have the largest populations.

The Islamic Saudi Academy in Alexandria, Virginia, enrolls almost 1,200 students in kindergarten through 12th grade. Although the school is funded by Saudi Arabia, Muslim children of any background can attend classes on the beautiful 100-acre campus. Some girls prefer to wear their traditional head scarves (hijab), while others do not. When participating on the basketball, volleyball, or soccer teams, the girls dress modestly in long pants instead of shorts. Both boys and girls sports teams are keen competitors with other private schools in the league.

Muslim Places of Worship

Muslims do not need a special place to worship as long as the area is clean. Places of worship have many different names, including church, synagogue, meeting house, temple, or ceremonial grounds. For Muslims, the official and preferred name is *masjid*, taken from the word *sajada*, which means to bend in worship. However, many people, particularly in non-Muslim countries, use the term *mosque*. In the United States, *mosque* is the most popular word.

Masjids can be simple open spaces or elaborate structures. They usually have a dome and at least one minaret, a tall slender tower with a balcony from which Muslims are summoned to prayer. In the past, a person called a *muadhin* or muezzin would climb to the top of the minaret and summon people to prayer with a special call called an *athan*. Today, the muezzin uses a microphone and loudspeaker system. Muslims pray five times daily; each prayer has its own special call. In masjids in the United States, the call to prayer is rarely broadcast outside. Dearborn,

Michigan, home of the country's largest masjid, is one of the few places in America where the call to prayer is made over a loudspeaker. In Muslim countries, the calls are heard throughout the town, and people mark time by them, much as people do with church bells ringing across the United States.

A masjid has an area for an imam, or prayer leader, and enough room for worshippers. They need space to stand in rows facing the city of *Makkah* (eastward) and to kneel and bend all the way to the floor from a kneeling position, showing humbleness. Worshippers can bring their own prayer rugs or use the carpeting available in the masjid. Masjids are often divided into a section for men in the front and a section for women in the back. Sometimes dividers and walls separate the areas, but it was not always this way. In Prophet Muhammad's time at the beginning of Islam, women sat in the back of the masjid with the children and men sat at the front, with no walls separating anyone from the imam. Women spoke directly to the Prophet, asking questions about religion or seeking advice. The masjid was a place of gathering and worship, but it was also a place where people interacted and discussed their daily lives.

Muslims, Christians, and Jews all worship the same universal God. The Arabic word for God is Allah or Al-Rub and is used by Arab Muslims, Jews, and Christians. All three groups believe their religions are descended from Abraham. Most Christians celebrate the holy day or Sabbath on Sunday. For Jews, it is from Friday night to Saturday. For Muslims, the holy day is Friday. Friday prayers are important gatherings. The word for Friday in Arabic is *Jumu'a*, from the word "to gather." Even though Muslims can worship at home,

they feel worshipping with others has greater merit. Merit is a system in which Muslims consider every deed in their lives to have the potential to gain them a better place in Paradise. Helping the elderly, orphans, and the poor are ways to get major merit points. But it's not only the big things that gain good points. Even small chores, like feeding a pet on time, smiling at someone, or opening the door for a person give a Muslim merit. By the same token, being mean or saying something negative to someone is a way to lose merit. Muslims believe that on the Day of Judgment, when everyone dies and leaves this life, the good deeds and the bad deeds are tallied. A person with more good deeds secures a place in Paradise (Heaven).

Play Mazen Al Qurani (The Hunter)

This Saudi Arabian game ("the hunter") is a combination of tag and hide-and-seek.

What You Need

Large open space

At least 4 friends

What You Do

1. Agree on where the boundaries of the game should be. Designate a safe place, or home, where the Hunter will base. If one steps outside the boundaries, he/she is automatically tagged. Decide who will be the Hunter.

2. The Hunter closes his or her eyes, faces a tree or building, and counts to 10. Everyone else runs and hides.

3. The Hunter finds, chases, and tags the other players before they can make it to home. If everyone is tagged, the first player who was caught becomes the Hunter. If the Hunter doesn't catch everyone, he or she shouts, "Clear and start over" and remains the Hunter.

Kuwait

Kuwait is a very small country that shares borders with Iraq and Saudi Arabia. It is mainly flat desert, with a coastline on the Arabian Gulf. The people are known for their hospitality and kindness to visitors. The Bedouin, an ethnic minority, are famous for their beautiful Sadu weavings. These tapestries, prized around the world for their designs and colors, were used for Bedouin tent homes and can withstand harsh desert climates. The Sadu House in Kuwait City preserves the craft and provides an outlet for Bedouin women to market their masterpieces.

For thousands of years the best pearls in the world came from the Arabian Gulf. At one time, pearls, not oil, were the main source of wealth in Kuwait. Pearl necklaces used to be quite the fashion accessory for American women. A pearl starts out like a splinter. Some type of foreign object slips into an oyster's shell, and the oyster surrounds it with a substance to stop the pain. The substance hardens, creating a perfect pearl!

The pearl industry lost much of its luster when oil was discovered in the area. Also, cultured pearl technology made it possible to "grow" pearls instead of hunting them from the sea bottom. But at one time, daring specialized divers would go miles out to sea on a boat called a dhow for months at a time. There were no diving suits and no SCUBA gear to protect them as they explored the depths of the ocean looking for oysters. Each diver had only a rope around his waist, a small basket around his neck to hold the oysters, and a clothespin to hold his nostrils shut to keep out the water. Divers had to be able to hold their breath for long periods of time. Sometimes a diver would hold a heavy rock to pull him down to the seabed. It was dangerous work—not only could they drown, but they were sometimes attacked by sea creatures.

Customs that developed around this perilous industry still exist today. In the old days, the families would gather on shore to send off the brave divers and also celebrate their return. A singer called a *nahham* would entertain the men on their long trips with sentimental songs about pearl diving. Today Kuwait hosts the Pearl Diving Festival, which celebrates all of the traditions around the pearl-diving industry, even going to sea to gather oysters, but only for one month. To prepare for this event, young divers take part in rigorous diving and sailing training taught by experienced divers and captains. It is a dying art, but the annual festivals keep this part of Kuwaiti history alive. And just as they were long ago, the divers are treated to a good meal when they return.

Stuff Date Candy

Dates are a sweet, delicious fruit from Arabia that grows on date palm trees. They are some of the world's oldest fruits, and there are different species and many stories about them. The famous phoenix bird was said to have always built its nest in the date palm before going up in flames and being reborn. Dates can be eaten fresh or dried.

What You Need

Adult supervision required

12 whole almonds

Frying pan

Wooden spatula

12 pitted Mejdool dates, or another kind of date

1 teaspoon ground cardamom

What You Do

1. Place the almonds in the frying pan over medium-low heat. Stir with a wooden spatula for about 2 minutes, or until you smell a fragrant roasting aroma. The almonds do not need to change color to be done. Set the almonds aside to cool.

2. Place one almond in each of the pitted dates. Sprinkle with ground cardamom and serve.

The Kuwait-America Foundation, based in Washington, DC, teams up with the National Campaign to Stop Violence to provide educational opportunities for poor and disadvantaged American children. More than 300,000 students have come up with solutions to end youth violence in the "Do the Write Thing Challenge." Their words have motivated thousands of adults across the country to volunteer their services to the program.

Oman

The legend of Sindbad is not just a fairy tale! Once upon a time there was a real "Sindbad the Sailor," and he was from Sohar, Oman. With the help of Omani ship builders in 1980, British author-explorer Timothy Severin built and sailed an authentic replica of Captain Sindbad's famous dhow. They named it *Sohar* and had a real adventure sailing from Oman to China in the ninth-century ship using navigational instruments that ancient Arab mariners had developed. The seven-month trip proved that early Arabs had astral navigation.

At one time Sohar was the capital of Oman (the current capital is Muscat), and it enjoyed a thriving copper trade. Today, it is a modern industrial city with a huge sports complex as well as museums where one can learn about the city's sailing traditions.

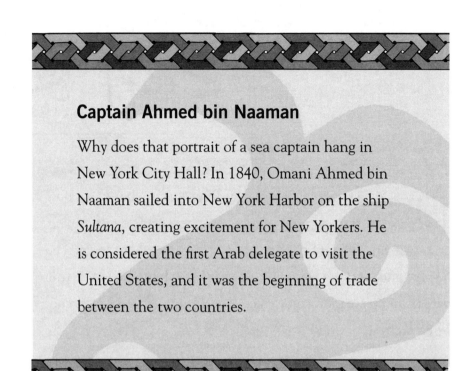

Captain Ahmed bin Naaman

Why does that portrait of a sea captain hang in New York City Hall? In 1840, Omani Ahmed bin Naaman sailed into New York Harbor on the ship *Sultana*, creating excitement for New Yorkers. He is considered the first Arab delegate to visit the United States, and it was the beginning of trade between the two countries.

The small nation of Oman borders Saudi Arabia, Yemen, and the United Arab Emirates. Oman is a beautiful country with a very long coastline that hugs the Arabian Sea, mountain ranges, deserts, and wadis (fertile valleys). Its economy is based on oil production and fishing. Like most others in the Arabian Gulf nations, most Omanis who come to the United States to study or work eventually return home.

Create Worry Beads

In times of stress, some Arab Americans may reach for a strand of worry beads. Sometimes called a *misbaha*, this way of calming the body and mind is popular throughout the Gulf countries. It is a way to put one's troubles in perspective. Worry beads may have come to the Middle East from India centuries ago. The strands have 33 or 99 beads, important numbers to both Christians and Muslims. Made of many different kinds of beads, there is always enough slack in the string so that, as each bead is held between the thumb and index finger and then released, it knocks against another bead with a click. The sound is very calming. Some say the practice of worry beads prevents people from forming bad habits such as smoking.

What You Need

24-inch-long strand of yarn or cording

36 faux pearl beads or other white beads, each with a hole large enough to string onto the cord

1 large bead, larger than the others, any shape

What You Do

1. String the beads onto the yarn, leaving a tail on each end at least 6 inches long. Tie the two ends together three times so you have a large knot.

2. String on the large bead and make sure it does not go beyond the knot. If it does, make the knot larger. Tie another knot on the other side of the large bead.

3. Unravel the yarn or cording ends so you have three strands. String a bead onto each and tie a knot to keep it from falling off.

4. Whenever you feel stressed or nervous, just focus on your beads. Grab, push, and release them one at a time, making sure they made a clicking noise. "Don't worry, be happy!"

The United Arab Emirates, Qatar, Bahrain

Gulf states have excellent relations with the United States. The United Arab Emirates, Qatar, and Bahrain are among the leading countries in providing work opportunities for US citizens.

The World Cup of football (soccer), sponsored by the International Federation of Association Football, will be held in Qatar in 2022 for the first time ever. American kids playing on soccer teams right now could very well grow up to be professional soccer players and part of the competition. Al Udeid Air Base, home to the US Air Force, is just west of Doha, the capital of Qatar. Georgetown University, located in our nation's capital of Washington, DC, also has a campus in Doha.

Texas A&M University has 14 branches in its college system. But did you know that one of them is in Qatar? At Texas A&M University in Education City, Qatar, students study engineering, but they also kick up their heels (and swords) in the Ardha martial arts folkdance. Warriors used to perform the Ardha before going into battle to show their bravery and to gain strength for the fight. Today the traditional sword dance is performed in Qatar on special occasions such as religious holidays, national celebrations, and college cultural festivals. Dancers face each other in two lines, and a poet gives each group of singers a line to repeat before moving to another group. The traditional lyrics are of loyalty and strength, and the drumming is loud and rhythmic. For centuries the drums of Ardha were used to declare war, swords were wielded, and poetry was recited, but today the Ardha is performed only for cultural appreciation. Besides drums, traditional ancient instruments like the *rabada* are used in this lively ancient dance.

The United Arab Emirates is a favorite destination for many travelers. This modern country of towering buildings features beautiful desert landscapes and water sports as well. The country is a federation of seven emirates, each very different from the others and each governed by an official called an emir. The most famous is Dubai, known for its big-city lifestyle. Many Americans live and work there. The capital of the UAE is Abu Dhabi, which is located north of Dubai.

From early December to early March, fleet-footed Arabians high step off jets to join in the fun in Dubai! Arabian American horses are there, too, neighing it up a bit in the lands from which their ancestors originated. The Dubai World Cup and Dubai International Arabian Horse Championship attract competitors from around the world. The famous Arabian horse breed was developed in Arab lands and is prized everywhere for its grace, beauty, and loyalty. It is said that the Arabian horse was the gift of Allah. Its bulging forehead held the blessings of God, its great arched neck was a sign of great courage, and the way the horse held its tail showed pride.

Bahrain is the smallest of the Arabian Gulf states, and although its oil reserves are few, it has a thriving refining business and is a leader in international banking services. In the modern capital city of Manama, the Museum of Pearl Diving features the history of the area's pearl-diving industry. Although there are not many Bahraini Americans, one North American Bahraini is very famous. Have you ever heard of the Tree of Life? The Tree of Life (Shajarat-al-Hayat) is a 400-year-old, 32-feet-high North American mesquite tree standing all alone in the heart of the desert, on top of a 25-foot-high sandy hill. It is very mysterious in many ways. No one knows how it got there. Scientists can't figure out how it survives, since no fresh water, above or below ground, exists in that area. All underground water sources around the tree are contaminated with salt. They think the tree may have developed a mutation to make it salt-tolerant. But local Bahrainis believe that the reason the tree has lived such a long time is because it is protected by Enki, the mythical god of water. They also believe that it marks the location of the Garden of Eden.

Say It in Kuwaiti

On happy occasions, Kuwaitis wish each other well by saying "Assakom Min Awwaddah," which means "happy returns."

ASSA-com min AWWA-dah. The A is pronounced like the a in *achoo*.

Girgian Candy Festival

Arabian Gulf people have many beautiful traditions. Families are very close knit, and extended families live in close proximity. It's not unusual for elderly parents to live with their children, forming strong bonds with their grandchildren.

One tradition is Girgian (also known as Garangaou and Haq Allah in some parts of the Gulf), a candy festival that is celebrated during the White Nights of Ramadan, the three days of the month before, during, and after the full moon. Since observant Muslims fast every day during Ramadan, the celebration takes place after the sunset meal. Children dress in traditional clothes and go from house to house. Singing is a fun part of Girgian, because they sing the Girgian song for candy, collecting it in bags they have decorated themselves before the occasion. Traditionally the children helped make sweets at home, but today store-bought candy is more popular. In the United States, families often hold Girgian parties at home instead of going door to door. The festival gets its name from the gurgling sound made by hard candy when it knocks against other candies in a bag.

Design a Girgian Candy Bag

You can make a candy bag, but it doesn't have to be just for candy. It can be a handy holder for all sorts of special objects. To make it really gurgle, add some hard candy and swing it around!

What You Need

2 index cards, 3 inches by 5 inches

Pencil

Ruler

Scissors

Plain canvas tote bag

Fabric markers in various colors

Fabric glue

Sequins in different colors

Bag of small faux pearls

What You Do

1. The Girgian bag will be decorated with a faux pearl dhow or boat. First, make the pattern for the sails. On one index card, draw a diagonal straight line from the top left-hand corner to the bottom right-hand corner. Cut out the two sails. Lay the sails on the table side by side.

2. The second index card will be the body of the dhow. Cut it into a trapezoid shape by cutting off the bottom corners. From the uncut top side of the card, cut two strips along the long side for the masts.

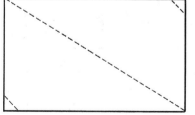 

3. Lay the canvas bag flat on a table and position the sails, mast, and body of the dhow at the center of the bag. Trace around them with the fabric marker. Now you will have a dhow on your bag.

4. Outline the dhow with glue and press on the faux pearls.

5. Fill the center of the dhow outline with glue and tamp down sequins so that the boat is totally filled in. Add any designs you wish with fabric markers.

6. Collect candy!

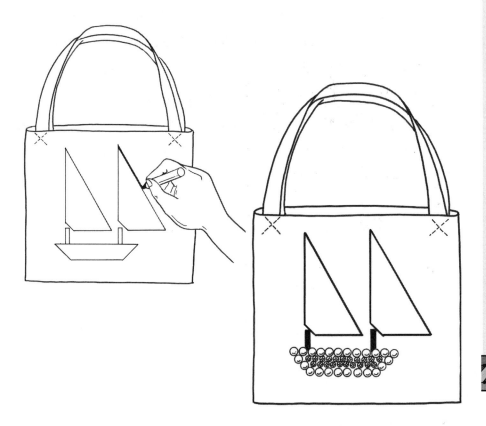

Notable Americans from Arabian Gulf Nations

Husain Abdulla (contemporary)   Activist and the director of Americans for Democracy and Human Rights in Bahrain.

Feryal Al-Masri (contemporary)   First Saudi American to run for US Congress. She teaches American History in Los Angeles, California.

Qusai Kheder (1978–)   Rapper who was educated in the United States. He became so popular that his hometown of Jeddah, Saudi Arabia, clamored for his return home.

Laila Al-Qatami (1970–)   First Arab American to be a board member of the American Civil Liberties Union. For several years, she was the communications director at the American-Arab Anti-Discrimination Committee.

❀ 10 ❀
From Admiral to Zero:
Celebrate the Arabic Heritage of America

Many states celebrate Arab American heritage by dedicating a month to honor Arab Americans. Because of the negative images in the media, it would seem that most people just don't like Arab Americans. But across the country, cities, schools, and libraries offer events that highlight the contributions that Arabs and Arab Americans have made to the world and to the United States. Arab Americans often hold festivals, or Mahrajans, which are like fairs and include fun activities and ethnic food. Celebrating the true story of Arab Americans helps to overcome hurtful discrimination and bias. The United States is a country made up of many different peoples who are all American. Libraries have featured really special programs—maybe because some of the world's first books were written in the Middle East!

But I Thought I Was Speaking English?

Did you know that countless English words are borrowed from other languages? These are called loan words, and many of them come from Arabic. Even many Spanish, French, and Latin words started as Arabic words, making them a double or triple loan to English. Can you imagine studying math without a "zero"? Speaking of math, "algebra" is an Arabic word, too! Trick-or-treating wouldn't be the same without "candy," and sleeping wouldn't be as comfortable without a "mattress," both from Arabic. Here are just a few English words and inventions on loan from Arabic.

alidade: a surveying instrument

almanac: *al-manāx*, the climate

amber: *anbar*, yellow

apricot: *al-birquq*

artichoke: *al-xurshūf*, the land thorn

caliber: *qâlib*, mould

carafe: *gharrāfa*, decanter

caramel: *kurat al milh*, ball of sweet salt

caraway: *karāwiya*

coffee: *qahwa*

cotton: *qutun*

crimson: *qirmazi* (possibly from the insect *qirmiz*, used to make red dye)

date: *daqal*, date palm

gazelle: *ghazal*

genie: Jinn

giraffe: *zarāfa*

henna: *hinna*

jar: *jarrah*, large earthen vase

jasmine: *yas(a)min*

lemon: *laymun*, all citrus fruit

lilac: *lilak*

lute: *al-ʕūd*, oud, ancestor of the guitar

monsoon: *mawsim*, season

muslin: from Mosul, Iraq, where cotton fabric was first made

orange: *naranj*

safari: *safar*, journey

safflower: *asfar*, yellow

sash: *shāsh*, wrap of muslin

satin: *zaytūnī*

scarlet: *siqillat*, fine cloth

sequin: *sikka*, coin

sherbet or syrup: *sharāb*, a drink

soda: *suwwāda*, a species of plant

spinach: *isfanakh*

sugar: *sukkar*

tahini: *taḥīn*, flour, derived from the Arabic verb for grind

tambourine: *tambur*

Coast to Coast in Arabic

Across the United States are towns with names from Arabic words or named after Middle Eastern people, cities, or countries. Places mentioned in the Bible are all in the region, and many US towns were given Biblical names. Elkader, Iowa, was founded in 1846 by Timothy Davis. He admired the international hero Emir Abd Elkader from Algeria, who rose up against French colonialism in his country in 1830. Today, Elkader is a sister city with Mascara, Algeria, birthplace of Emir Elkader. Here are just a few of the many towns with Arabic names. You can keep an eye out for Arabic-inspired architecture, which is very common in the Americas.

Aladdin, Wyoming

Alexandria, Virginia

Bagdad, California

Bethlehem, Pennsylvania

Cairo, Illinois

Twelve states have a Damascus:
   Alabama, Arkansas,
   Georgia, Illinois, Maryland,
   Maine, New York, Ohio,
   Oregon, Pennsylvania,
   Tennessee, Virginia

Egypt, Pennsylvania

Jordan, Pennsylvania

Lebanon, South Dakota
   (and many other states)

Mecca, California

Medina, Ohio (previously
   called Mecca)

Memphis, Tennessee

Nebo, North Carolina

New Jerusalem, Pennsylvania

Palestine, Texas

Syria, Virginia

Tripoli, Iowa

Chef Jeffrey Saad (1967–)

Meal sharing is a major part of Arabic cultures. Many suburban families take lengthy car trips into cities just so they can buy the freshest and most authentic ingredients. Some grandmothers may still rule the kitchen, which is often considered the center of the home, just as it was generations ago. But Chef Saad made it into the kitchen and grew up around his sitti (grandmother), who made stuffed grape leaves and other tasty fare. Like her grandson, she was also famous for her cooking and was even featured in the *Chicago Tribune* food section.

Jeffrey thinks he could probably recognize the smell of cardamom before he could walk! The Food Network star, born in 1967, grew up in the Chicago, Illinois, suburb of Hinsdale. Not only did he study culinary arts in college, he also interned with some of the world's most famous chefs. Besides hosting *United Tastes of America*, Jeffery is also the spokesperson for the "Incredible Edible Egg." He believes in "cooking locally and eating globally," which means using food grown close to home, as it will be cheaper and fresher. As a dad, he likes to prepare Sitti's famous Puffy Pancakes with his kids.

Cook Sitti's Puffy Pancakes

When Jeffrey was growing up, he used to go to his grandparents' lake house in Wisconsin, called the House of Seven Gables. He remembers it as a special time, as all the cousins would gather from around the country and sleep in one big room in the gables. At night, they all fell asleep to laughter, and in the morning, the children woke up to the smell of the puffy pancake his grandmother made in her ancient cast iron pan. Jeffrey says that the smell of sweet butter and caramelized sugar still makes him think of Sitti!

What You Need

Adult supervision required

Oven

½ cup butter

Cast iron frying pan

Mixing bowl

2 eggs

2 tablespoons sugar

½ cup milk

½ cup flour

Spoon

Maple syrup, jelly, honey,
  or other syrup

Makes four servings

What You Do

1. Preheat the oven to 400°F. Add the butter to the pan and place it in the oven.

2. In a mixing bowl, mix together the eggs, sugar, milk, and flour. A few small lumps are OK; don't overmix the batter.

3. When the butter has melted and turned golden brown in the pan, remove it from the oven. Immediately pour the batter into the pan and return it to the oven.

4. Bake until golden mountains form (about 15 minutes). Make sure everyone is standing around when you pull it out of the oven, as the mountains turn to valleys quickly!

5. Cut into serving-sized pieces and pour your favorite syrup or topping on top. Enjoy!

Find out if your town or library recognizes Arab American Heritage Month. If so, you can join in by sharing some of the activities in this book. If not, maybe you can get some friends together and start a celebration. You can cook up some of the recipes and play games featured in this book. Make some displays showing Arab American people and their contributions and, of course, dance the dabkeh while keeping the beat on the riq and derbekke.

Design a Banner for Arab American Heritage Month with Arabic Calligraphy

Arabic calligraphy is Arabic writing that has taken on an artistic quality. Arabic is the language of the Qur'an, the Muslim holy book. Because Muslims feel it is disrespectful to create art that represents humans or living things, they began to use calligraphy to decorate places of worship and homes and to beautify the pages of the Qur'an. Calligraphers spend many years perfecting their art and working under the supervision of masters of the craft. There are four main types of calligraphy, each with its own features.

Try your hand at this centuries-old art form using the English alphabet.

What You Need

Roll of plain shelf paper

Scissors

1 carpenter pencil (or another really big pencil)

1 regular pencil

Masking tape

Markers

Magazines

Photographs from the Internet

Glue

Choice of decorations

What You Do

1. Roll out the shelf paper to your desired length and cut.

2. Tape the pencils together so that the points are level.

3. Write "Arab American Heritage Month" across the banner with the pencils. Make the writing as fancy as you like. Color in between the lines with the markers.

4. Make a collage on the banner with pictures of different Arab Americans. Decorate your banner however you like and attach it to a wall with masking tape.

Resources

Arab American Museums, Festivals, and Cultural Centers

Almost every state has at least one Arab American festival or Mahrajan. Just a few are listed here.

California

Annual Arab American Day Festival
Arab American Council
518 South Brookhurst Street, Suite 5
Anaheim, CA 92804
(714) 758-3507
www.aafestival.com

This annual festival is usually held in the latter part of September and celebrates Arab American cultures and Arab countries. Started in 1995, the festival features food, dancing, music, art, and poetry.

Kan Zaman
P.O. Box 661551
Arcadia, CA 91066-1551
(626) 432-8235
www.kanzaman.org/index.html

The Kan Zaman Community Ensemble teaches and performs all types of Arabic music.

Sam and Alfreda Maloof Foundation for Arts and Crafts
5131 Carnelian Street
Alta Loma, CA 91701
(909) 980-0412
www.malooffoundation.org/

This living museum features the art of Sam Maloof, one of America's finest woodworkers and a leader of the California modern arts movement.

Florida

The Arab American Community Center (AACC)

    of Central Florida

4540 W. Colonial Drive

Orlando, FL 32808

(407) 504-7333

www.aaccflorida.org/

www.arabamericanculturalfestival.org/Tampa/

    This organization sponsors one of the largest Arab festivals in the South: Arab Festival Tampa.

Michigan

American Arab Chamber of Commerce

12740 W. Warren Avenue, Suite 300

Dearborn, MI 48126

(313) 945-1700

www.americanarab.com/

    The American Arab Chamber of Commerce sponsors the country's largest Arab American Festival, held in Dearborn, Michigan. Every year the festival attracts almost 400,000 people who enjoy rides, games, feasting, performances, and contests.

Arab American National Museum

13624 Michigan Avenue

Dearborn, MI 48126

(313) 582-AANM (2266)

www.arabamericanmuseum.org/

    Affiliated with the Smithsonian, the Arab American National Museum (AANM) is the first and only museum in the United States devoted to Arab American history and culture. Changing and permanent exhibits feature the diversity of Arab Americans, Arab American history, and the Arab American experience.

Chaldean Cultural Center

5600 Walnut Lake Road

West Bloomfield, MI 48323

(248) 681-5050

www.chaldeanculturalcenter.org/index.html

    The Cultural Center/Museum features the history of Chaldeans in the Middle East and the United States. Special cultural and language programs are offered to kids and adults.

Nevada

Lebanese American Festival
St. Sharbel Mission of Las Vegas
10325 Rancho Destino Road
Las Vegas, NV 89183
(702) 616-6902
www.lebaneseamericanfestivallasvegas.org/

This annual festival features all things Lebanese.

New Hampshire

Mahrajan Middle Eastern Festival
Our Lady of Cedars Melkite Church
140 Mitchell Street
Manchester, NH 03103
www.mahrajan-nh.com/

Arabic food, dancing, and Josh the Camel brighten up this annual festival.

New York

Alwan for the Arts
16 Beaver Street, 4th Floor
New York, NY 10004
(646) 732-3261
www.alwanforthearts.org/

Alwan for the Arts showcases the diverse cultures of Arab Americans and Arabs. They offer film festivals and screenings, book and poetry readings and signings, lectures and conferences, art exhibits, musical and theatrical performances, and language and literature classes and festivals.

Moroccan American House Association
7304 5th Avenue, PMB #246
Brooklyn, New York 11209
http://moroccanamericanhouse.com/

The Association offers cultural activities for children and adults as well as Arabic language lessons.

New York Arabic Orchestra
www.newyorkarabicorchestra.org/index.html

Founded in 2007, the Orchestra performs contemporary and classical Arabic music and features a culturally diverse group of professional musicians who play Arabic music.

Ohio

Syrian Gardens

Cleveland Cultural Gardens Federation

750 East 88th Street

Cleveland, OH 44108-1285

(216) 367-9130

http://culturalgardens.org/gardenDetail.aspx?gardenID=18

Opened in 2011, the gardens pay homage to thousands of Syrian-Lebanese Americans in the Cleveland area. A beautifully designed outdoor space, it features symbols of Syria and of Syrians in America.

Oregon

Arab American Cultural Center of Oregon

1332 S.W. Custer Drive

Portland, Oregon 97219

www.araboregon.org/

The Arab American Cultural Center of Oregon (AACCO) promotes the heritage of Oregon's diverse Arab American community. AACCO hosts an annual Mahrajan festival.

Pennsylvania

Al-Bustan Seeds of Culture

526 South 46th Street

Philadelphia, PA 19143

(267) 809-3668

http://albustanseeds.org

Al-Bustan Seeds of Culture is dedicated to teaching and presenting Arab arts and culture. The Arab Music Concert Series features world-renowned Arab and Arab American musicians as well as the Philadelphia Arab Music Ensemble, an orchestra of local musicians. They offer a summer culture and language camp for elementary through high school kids and give classes in Arabic singing and percussion instruments.

Berber American Community

P.O. Box 54928

Philadelphia, PA 19148

www.berber-american.org

The Berber American Community (BAC) promotes Berber culture and the Amazigh language.

Tennessee

Salahadeen Center of Nashville
364 Elysian Fields Court
Nashville, TN 37211
(615) 333-0530
http://scntn.org/home2
   The center offers support and cultural programs for the Muslim and Kurdish community.

Texas

Arab-American Cultural and Community Center
10555 Stancliff Road
Houston TX, 77099
(832) 351-3366
www.acc.houston.org
   The Arab-American Cultural and Community Center offers a wide range of services, including cultural programs, Arabic language lessons, resources on Arab Americans, and a museum featuring the Arab American history of Texas.

Washington, DC

Kahlil Gibran Memorial Garden
3100 Massachusetts Avenue, NW
Washington DC, 20008
   The Kahlil Gibran Memorial Garden was founded in 1991 to celebrate the 100th anniversary of the poet's birth.

West Virginia

Our Lady of Lebanon Church
2216 Eoff Street
Wheeling, WV 26003
(304) 233-1688
The church sponsors an annual Mahrajan festival.

Wisconsin

Arab World Festival
P.O. Box 517
Milwaukee, WI 53201-0517
(888) 912-2722
   Arab World Fest is a yearly festival held on Milwaukee's lakefront, celebrating the music, food, and culture of the 22 Middle Eastern countries.

Suggested Reading List for Kids

Abdel-Fattah, Randa. *Where the Streets Had a Name*. New York: Scholastic, 2010.

Abdu, Rashid. *Journey of a Yemeni Boy*. Pittsburgh, PA: Dorrance Publishing Co., Inc., 2005.

Addasi, Maha. *Time to Pray*. Honesdale, PA: Boyds Mill Press, 2010.

———. *White Nights of Ramadan*. Honesdale, PA: Boyds Mill Press, 2008.

Ashabranner, Brent. *An Ancient Heritage: The Arab American Minority*. New York: HarperCollins, 1991.

Awad, Abed, and Patrice Samara. *Alphabet Kids—Umar's Magic Oven*. New York: Alphabet Kids, 2010.

Awde, Nicholas, and Putros Samano. *The Arabic Alphabet: How to Read and Write It*. New York: Kennsington, 2000.

Bahous, Sally. *Sitti and the Cats*. Lanham, MD: Roberts Rinehart, 1997.

Barakat, Ibtisam. *Tasting the Sky: A Palestinian Childhood*. New York: Farrar Straus Giroux, 2007.

Boueri, Marijean. *Lebanon 1-2-3: A Counting Book in Three Languages*. Exeter, NH: Pub Works, 2005.

Bowers, Aisha. *Fun in the Emirates*. London: Motivate Publishing Ltd., 2011.

———. *Fun in the Gulf*. London: Motivate Publishing Ltd., 2011.

Bunting, Eve. *One Green Apple*. New York: Clarion, 2006.

Dennis, Yvonne Wakim, and Arlene Hirschfelder. *Children of the U.S.A.* Watertown, MA: Charlesbridge Press, 2008.

Letts, Elizabeth, and Ali Alalou. *The Butter Man*. Watertown, MA: Charlesbridge Press, 2011.

Marston, Elsa. *Santa Claus in Baghdad and Other Stories about Teens in the Arab World*. Bloomington, IN: Indiana University Press, 2008.

———. *The Ugly Goddess*. Peru, IL : Cricket Books, 2002.

———. *The Phoenicians*. Tarrytown, NY. Marshall Cavendish, 2001.

———. *The Ancient Egyptians*. Tarrytown, NY. Marshall Cavendish, 2005.

———. *The Lebanese in America*. Minneapolis: Learner, 1987.

Matze, Claire Sidhom. *The Stars in My Geddoh's Sky*. Park Ridge, IL: Albert Whitman & Company, 2002.

Munsch, Robert, and Saoussan Askar, *From Far Away*. Buffalo, NY: Annick Press, 1995.

Naff, Alixa. *The Arab-Americans*. New York: Chelsea House Publishers, 1988.

Nye, Naomi Shihab. *Habibi*. New York: Simon & Schuster, 1999.

———. *Honeybee: Poems and Short Prose*. New York: Greenwillow Press, 2008.

———. *A Maze Me: Poems for Girls*. New York: HarperCollins, 2005.

———. *Sitti's Secrets*. New York: Simon & Schuster, 1994.

Shefelman, Janice. *A Peddler's Dream*. Boston: Houghton Mifflin, 1992.

Stanley, Diane. *Saving Sky*. New York: HarperCollins, 2010.

Steffens, Bradley *Ibn al-Haytham: First Scientist*. Greensboro, NC: Morgan Reynolds, 2007.

Turhan, Sedat. *Milet Picture Dictionary: English-Arabic*. Chicago: Milet Publishing, 2003.

Whitesides, Barbara. *Sugar Comes from Arabic*. Northampton, MA: Interlink, 2009.

Wolf, Bernard. *Coming to America: A Muslim Family's Story*. New York: Lee and Low, 2003.

Suggested Reading List for Adults

Ameri, Anan. *Arab American Reference Library: Encyclopedia*. Farmington Hills, MI: UXL, 1999.

Arab American Institute. "Healing the Nation: The Arab American Experience after September 11, 2001." Washington, DC: Arab American Institute, 2002. http://aai.3cdn. net/64de7330dc475fe470_h1m6b0yk4.pdf.

Barakat, Halim. *The Crane*. Washington, DC: Jerusalem Fund, 2008.

Bayoumi, Moustafa. *How Does It Feel to Be a Problem? Being Young and Arab in America*. New York: Penguin, 2008.

Curiel, Jonathan. *Al' America: Travels Through America's Arab and Islamic Roots*. New York: New Press, 2008.

Haiek, Joseph. *Arab American Almanac*, 6th Edition. Glendale, CA: News Circle Publishing House, 2010.

Kayal, Philip, and Kathleen Benson. *A Community of Many Worlds: Arab Americans in New York City*. Syracuse, NY: Syracuse University Press, 2002.

Kayyali, Randa A. *The Arab Americans*. Santa Barbara, CA: ABC-CLIO, 2006.

Malek, Alia. *A Country Called Amreeka*. New York: Simon & Schuster, 2009.

Orfalea, Gregory. *The Arab Americans: A History*. Northampton, MA: Olive Branch Press, 2006.

Said, Edward. *Out of Place*. New York: Knopf, 1999.

Shaheen, Jack G. *Reel Bad Arabs: How Hollywood Vilifies a People*. Northampton, MA: Olive Branch Press, 2009.

Shora, Nawar. *The Arab-American Handbook: A Guide to the Arab, Arab-American and Muslim Worlds*. Seattle, WA: Cune Press, 2009.

Zogby, James. *Arab Voices: What They Are Saying to Us, and Why It Matters*. New York: Palgrave Macmillan, 2010.

Websites

ACCESS: www.accesscommunity.org/site/PageServer?pagename =homepage.

Alkitab: www.alkitab.com.

Amazigh Cultural Association in America (ACAA), Inc.: www.tamazgha.org/index.html.

Arab American and Chaldean Council: www.myacc.org.

Arab and Chaldean Festival: www.arabandchaldeanfestival.com.

American Arab Forum: www.aafusa.org/index.htm.

American-Arab Anti-Discrimination Committee: www.adc.org.

American Druze Society: www.druze.com.

Arab America: www.arabamerica.com/arabamericans.php.

Arab American Historical Foundation: www.arabamerican history.org.

Arab American Institute: www.aaiusa.org.

Arab World and Islamic Resources: www.awaironline.org /index.html.

Association of Patriotic Arab Americans in the Military: www.apaam.org.

Chaldean Federation: www.chaldeanfederation.org.

Council on American-Islamic Relations (CAIR): www.cair.com.

Cynthia Leitich Smith: www.cynthialeitichsmith.com.

Helen Zughaib: www.hzughaib.com.

Interlink Books: www.interlinkbooks.com

Jack Hanna: www.jackhanna.com.

Khayrallah Program for Lebanese-American Studies: http://faculty .chass.ncsu.edu/akhater/lac.

Ladah Foundation: palestinianembroider.tripod.com.

Lebanese Books: www.lebanesebooks.com/Merchant2 /merchant.mvc?.

Middle Eastern American Resources Online: www.mearo.org.

Middle East Outreach Center: www.meoc.us/about.

National Apostolate of Maronites: www.namnews.org/index .php?page=parisheslist.

Radius of Arab American Writers: www.rawi.org.

Saudi Aramco World Magazine: www.saudiaramcoworld.com/about.us.

Seeds of Peace: www.seedsofpeace.org.

Syraj: www.syraj.com.

Index